The NOWING® Formula

The NOWING® Formula

How Millennials can maximize their professional
performance and stay healthy in the digital era

Michaela Lindinger

ISBN: 1530377781
ISBN 13: 9781530377787
Library of Congress Control Number: 2016904167
CreateSpace Independent Publishing Platform
North Charleston, South Carolina

This book is dedicated to my Mama, who was the most loving teacher a child could ask for; my wonderful husband, Christian, who is the best companion for my happy life; and my adorable daughter, Leona, who shall enjoy a life full of passion, performance, and well-being in the future of the digital economy.

Table of Contents

Free resources
for you

Visit **braininspa.com** to get these free resources:

Download your free resource work sheets including exercises for each NOWING® chapter in the book. This practical booklet will support you over the course of reading this book and help to bring structure to the exercises.

Complete the individual NOWING® questionnaire and receive a complimentary personal guide to more performance, productivity, and health.

Access all of the above free resources at braininspa.com. They will be available for only a limited time, so get your free copies today.

Let us realize that it is the moment that counts.
Not the YESTERDAY.
Not the TOMORROW.
But the NOW.

[Michaela Lindinger, 2003]

One

Recently at 36,000 feet

That's too much for me—this shared, digital disruptive something. I don't even know what to do with all the real-time information available, connected technologies, virtual collaboration...

> *It sounds as if you were introduced to the new digital industry.*

I have read about the digital transformation and the rise of new business models, but I was confident that this didn't have anything to do with my company—I mean, we have been market leaders since 1985, our products are superb, and our global expansion went really well in the last decades...till last year...

> *So what happened that caused you trouble?*

I have no clue where to start—it was this new company, a start-up that came out of nowhere with a service-focused business model and a strong online channel, and all of a sudden my figures were down 30 percent, and the best talents on my team left to go work for other companies where they "found more meaning and a better work-life blend." That's crazy, isn't it?

> *Well, there is a new generation of millennial talent who don't work and perform like their parents did. Their motivation is different; so is their skill set and their style of working.*

"Performance"—that's the key word. I have no idea how I should improve my team's performance without going nuts, nor do I have a clue how to attract good talent for my company or how to retain the talent I still have…and I haven't had much time for my private life and my health lately, so it would be nice to find a magic formula…

> *Well, there is hardly ever a magic formula that allows for "no input and maximum output." But if you are serious and willing to put forth some effort, I can show you a formula that has worked quite well for many.*

All right, the flight is thirty more minutes, so tell me all I need to know about this formula that can get my performance and my health back to high levels despite this digital economy.

Two

Foreword

I would like to start this foreword by quoting what Michaela wrote in her final chapter that resonates with me: "I feel truly honored that our paths have crossed and that I had the privilege to share my passion and some of my personal insights with..." people who aspire to learn and acquire the mastery of living their dreams. I came across Michaela when she was conducting her research about real drivers for motivation, high performance, and health of millennials and as I supervised her research dissertation. At the time I was impressed by Michaela's own standard of performance, and it was not surprising that her dissertation achieved distinction and was selected as an example of the best dissertation of the year. I am now pleasantly surprised that Michaela has further developed the NOWING® Formula, and I read the manuscript with joy. It is packed with sound advice and ideas that are grounded in evidence-based research and practice yet is easy for the layperson to read and is free of academic jargon or psychobabble. Reading the text, I believe she has brought the narrative alive by taking us through a journey that is based on her personal lived experience as a young executive in the world of international business, as a coaching psychologist, and as a millennial working mother and family manager.

So to conclude this foreword, I would like to say that I feel not only honored and privileged but also very proud and humbled to read and learn that my former student could communicate her learning and practical wisdom with such eloquence and maturity that bridges the generational gap. As Confucius said, "Learning has no front-runner or latecomer; the one who arrives (to the true knowledge) is the first."

I, for one—even though I am from generation X—can take a chapter from this book and implement it in my everyday life. I am sure that you, as a reader from generation X, Y, or Z, can also benefit from this, right here and NOW. Enjoy.

Dr. Ho Law, PhD

Coaching Program Adviser to the University of Cambridge, UK

Founder of Empsy®, Cambridge Coaching Psychology Group,

Chartered Scientist, Psychologist, Manager, Registered Psychologist,

Fellow of the Higher Education Academy; Fellow of the Royal Society

of Medicine; Associate Fellow of British Psychological Society

Three

Welcome

Have you noticed the change, the disruption, the newness that is in the air—or should we say "in the cloud"? There is currently a digital transformation taking place, and we are driving at three hundred miles per hour toward a world of connected everything. Shared. Me. Digital. Disruptive. Real-time. Big. Agile. The lines between business and private life are blurred, and that has an impact on individuals in leadership positions, on young professionals, and on talents like you.

In my previous role in the corporate world, I was responsible for something called "value creation and innovation services" for several countries within central Europe. It was my job to help large global corporations across industries to answer their most strategic questions with regard to this new digital industry and all its challenges: a truckload of conversations, workshops, team discussions, facilitated innovation jams, and many meetings in which all participants circled around the question of what the new technological advancements and opportunities mean. How could they leverage them in the best possible way for their own company? In all those conversations, it became crystal clear that technology is essential for mastering this disruptive digital shift. It also became apparent that today's technological opportunities can support almost any creative idea from a talented individual or team. Finally, it was evident that it would never be technology alone that leads to great innovations:

The #1 factor allowing companies to achieve great innovative breakthroughs is the abilities of their talent, the performance of healthy, motivated individuals who make the difference in a company's future success or failure.

There is a chain reaction we are all aware of: innovative, differentiating, great ideas and concepts come from great minds at the peak of their performance. And the basis for high performance is not only know-how and motivation but also a handful of other factors, most importantly a healthy setting for individual well-being.

Although our lives are quite different compared to those of people who lived a thousand years ago, our DNA hasn't changed that much: we are still human beings who need to rest, relax, spend time outside work with family and friends, and engage in physical activity to recharge our batteries in order to deliver high performance in our demanding digital world. So a key question we all face at some point is this: How can I increase my performance—which is necessary to survive, remain challenged, and deliver innovative ideas in today's professional world—while improving my health, which is even more important to survive and to enjoy life with my family and friends for as long as possible?

For the last several years, it has been my personal mission to help young talent, entrepreneurs, organizations, and visionary professionals do exactly that: increase performance and improve health in order to enjoy more clarity, be more influential and productive, and have more success. Any form of high performance—whether it is from an individual or an entire organization—can be achieved and sustained fully only if it takes well-being into consideration.

In more than ten years as one of the youngest executives in a global management-consulting firm, I have worked with different management levels across cultures and helped international organizations on their transformation journey. My projects took me from the north of Russia to the south of Italy, from Hong Kong to New York City, and to almost all the countries in Central Europe. I have seen teams and leaders embracing industry disruption and digital challenges with excitement and curiosity. I spent my days with Fortune 500 companies, helping them achieve innovative breakthroughs for the digital industry. I have seen the difference between high-performing, healthy teams and those squeezed like lemons and pushed like doorbells until the entire team or individuals fell apart. Burned out. Gone.

My own industry experience helps me understand the burning platforms, the needs, and the challenges faced by professionals and young talent in the corporate world. My academic background in international business and my research in coaching psychology with a focus on leadership and health of generation Y provide me with the know-how and the tools needed for helping millennial talents perform at their best and still improve their well-being.

Most importantly, however, I am a millennial myself, married and a mother to a wonderful little daughter. I know personally how great it is to have a highly successful, fast-progressing career according to my vision but also a private life with enough time for my family, friends, and my lovely English garden in the middle of the Austrian countryside.

During all those years in the corporate world, many professionals shared with me their frustrations about their current situation:

- *"In my daily job I am constantly expected to over-achieve, dealing with increased cost and time pressure, day in and day out."*

- *"My family and friends are the most important network and my true source of energy, but I feel that excessive work demands are not worth the sacrifices in my private life."*

- *"I should have seriously questioned all the mountains of deadlines, meetings, and reports before I had my heart attack. Luckily, I survived, and now I am not so sure if all this was really worth the sacrifices in my private life."*

- *"I am lacking efficient personal-development initiatives, immediate feedback, and a good balance of skill and challenge, and there is nobody supporting me to transfer know-how from training into my daily operations. Is this the place they call work?"*

- *"The environment that allows ideas and opportunities to emerge, making discussions and reflections possible, helping to define a strategic road map to my personal high performance—this environment is simply missing."*

- *"We are talking about new business models, disrupting technologies, and the impact of digital on our company. But we never touch the human factor in this equation. What a shame. This won't lead to urgently needed innovative new products."*

The good news is that it doesn't have to be this way for you. There are proven, practical solutions and simple tools available to raise an organization's readiness for the digital era and to lift the individual players in this digital game up to their best levels. We are the actors in this digital game, and we need to be trained in a short period of time to reach the top level we all deserve, with tools and exercises that are effective and suitable for a digital lifestyle.

Numerous models have touched on the topic of achieving high performance from different angles, and about as many list what's needed for a healthy, satisfying life. There is also a plethora of books explaining the upcoming talents of generation Y and the challenges presented by the new digital industry. However, none of these documents or models have brought all those essential elements together and answered the key question:

How can millennial talents and young professionals increase their performance and improve their health in the digital industry in order to achieve innovative solutions and remain fully motivated?

The model to help answer this most critical question is the NOWING® Formula. At its heart is the understanding that everything we do is not about yesterday or tomorrow but about today, about being here and now. This formula helps one to achieve more clarity, productivity, motivation, and presence as well as a much lower stress level. Subsequently, an individual's mental balance, well-being, and overall health can improve, leading to levels of individual success and energy never experienced before.

This book is about the NOWING® Formula. It will help you raise the bar of your personal performance and your health.

You will love this because after reading these pages and applying only half of the exercises, tips, and secrets explained, you will be capable of performing way above the norm, with better results and much more influence on others. And chances are high that you will see significant improvements in your health and well-being. There is absolutely no need to be part of the mediocre crowd if you have the chance to join the club of high performers and super achievers.

I believe you would love to have a great professional career and still have valuable time for your family.

I believe that a healthy body **and** a clear mind are the only tickets to sustainable success and a joyful life.

I believe you can make easy changes today that help boost your productivity and bring you closer to your life's dream.

I believe that life is not about yesterday or tomorrow; it is about the here and now.

Therefore, I invite you to take a look behind the curtain of what performance in this digital industry is all about, what you really need to do to become an admired, healthy, high performer, and which steps you should take for a journey to the top level that you deserve.

Welcome to the world of NOWING®.

Four

The digital game

MY GAME WASN'T ALWAYS WIN-WIN

Yes, I am a millennial myself. I was raised in a middle-class Austrian family in the countryside. Most of my childhood days were spent outside, in beautiful nature, having fun with children from the neighborhood. I was blessed with an existing and functioning family network, grandparents who had a little farm, and traditions playing an important role in my family's life. I grew up in relationships filled with love, and there were always a handful of trusted people around me. The most important person in my life as a child and teenager was my Mama: the two of us had one of those relationships that you can only have with a person who truly and unconditionally loves you, who is open and honest, and who is thankful to God for being alive every day. Thanks to her, I had the chance to have a stable childhood, which led to me becoming a grounded person and knowing the importance of being present.

Performance has always been essential in my life—maybe because I learned in my early childhood that I could improve my situation if I pushed and challenged myself to reach the next level, and if I truly believed in myself I could achieve a lot with time, energy, and commitment. It started out with simple things, such as straight As in my first years of school—I know most of you had that. For me as a girl from the countryside, these grades resulted in going to a private school in a nearby city instead of staying at the small local school. The life in the nearby city was good and exposed me to different people and different perspectives. It was my performance in the first six years at this private school that allowed me to skip a class in the seventh year and spend an entire year as an exchange student in the United States at the age of sixteen. Even there I managed to optimize my academic performance to a level at which I was allowed to participate in college courses of advanced anatomy and physiology, receiving an offer for a medical-school scholarship from one of my professors—which I turned down because I wasn't ready to stay in the United States at the age of sixteen without my family and friends—yes, I am being fully honest with you here.

Back home in Austria it was again only my commitment and strong will for hard work that made it possible to complete my high school graduation in Austria with distinction despite skipping this one year in the United States. I then enjoyed a great time at university, spending a semester abroad at an Asian Ivy League college thanks to a performance scholarship. At the peak of my incipient career, in my last semester at university I got an offer (because of a great student project I had done for free) for a paid internship in New York City as the assistant to the chief financial officer of one of the world's largest logistics service providers. Being a millennial myself, at the age of twenty-one, I found this to be an awesome challenge.

But all of a sudden things changed dramatically. In my office in New York City one day during my internship program, I got a phone call at nine thirty in the morning from Mama, who was fighting cancer back home. Mama told me on the phone that she thought this was the last time we would talk, telling me how much she loved me and that we would always be together in our hearts, even if we couldn't see or touch each other anymore. She wanted me to keep up my good spirits and my high performance, and she reminded me not to forget to make something out of my life. The next thing I remember was getting on the next available flight from New York City to Vienna because I desperately wanted to see and hug her again, maybe for the last time.

And while I was on the plane, thousands of feet over the ocean, Mama died.

I had no chance for one last big hug. No chance for one last sentence face-to-face that she would still hear. No chance for one final touch. I knew from this moment on that my biggest fan, my greatest adviser, the one and only person I trusted fully and who loved me unconditionally was gone. Gone forever.

There is no need to describe the misery I felt, all the pain I was going through. Within a second, my great career prospects after college were not important anymore. There were only two things that kept me alive back then: one was the promise I had given Mama on the phone that I would make something out of my life and that I would remain a happy person, and the second was my constant repetition of Mama's key message: "If there is one thing I want to make sure you take into your heart, it is that you know life is not about yesterday or about tomorrow; it is about today, about being here and now."

After Mum's death I initially lost direction, and there was not much performance or health in my life. Obviously the road back was a tough one, but I managed to finish my studies and applied for an analyst job at one of the biggest global consulting firms. Yes, I could have done something less challenging, something more local and easier to manage with the skill set I had. But my drive for performance was back again, and I started to dive into tons of work, following a fast-track consulting career, raising my annual salary more than 400 percent in just a few years. Things went well for me business-wise, but my life wasn't serving my real passion. I was not fully enjoying the moment. I was always either worrying about tomorrow or thinking about what had happened yesterday, what others thought of me, and whether I could trust those around me. Expectations of my performance were extremely high, as were my workload and the hours I spent week after week, night after night for my clients, my team, and my company. Performing at this level made me an "optimization" guru: I would try any productivity-improvement method or self-efficiency tool; any new or old technique for remaining a well-balanced person despite sixty-hour workweeks; any physical or mental workout that would help me boost my brainpower; any formula that would support me in being more influential, a better team leader, or communicating with my clients more successfully. Career-wise, things paid off: I was getting fast-track promotions and moved from analyst to one of the youngest members of the executive team in just a few years. But something deep inside was missing. And it was so hard for me not to have Mama as my best, most trusted adviser to talk about that missing piece.

It took some years after Mama's death before things changed again: I got married to the love of my life, the one man who had been with me since those tough days when Mama left, who had been the best companion through the roller-coaster ride during my consulting career, and who promised on our wedding day in a beautiful castle by a small lake in Upper Austria to stay with me till the end of my life. A year after we got married, I was blessed by giving birth to a little baby girl, now being a Mama myself. On one hand, this new role was an amazingly wonderful experience, but on the other hand, it brought up the pain of not having my own Mama to ask all the big questions you have as a young mother. Even worse, I was sad and mad at the same time that my daughter would never know her wonderful, loving grandma.

At work I also had to cope with how everyone expected me to perform as I had at previous levels. But I wanted to raise a little girl who was and still is my most precious jewel in life. As a result, my private and business life goals started colliding, and I knew I had to take the big lessons learned from Mama to the next level and really incorporate them into my personal daily life. I knew I desperately wanted to get some work-life blend back and stay healthier to serve my daughter and my little family as long as God allowed me to do so.

I wanted to understand and investigate extensively what had allowed me to continue my successful career after all that pain with Mama's early death. I was also curious about how I could become even better at living her message about being here and now. What would it take that I had already done right to get going again? I wanted to learn more about what latest research and insights were out there that I could apply in living my life more fully, in a more balanced way, and above all in a healthier way while still enjoying professional success, a great career, and working toward my true passion.

I also knew that there were other young professionals out there who had experienced a similar personal tragedy, who had gone through a similar misery, and I wanted to help them find the best way through those tough times, back to healthy high performance, by applying my experience.

Despite having my first master's degree in international business, I decided to go for a second master's degree in psychology, learning more about the psyche, motivation, physical and emotional health, stress and its effect on performance, and discovery of the unconscious to find one's true strengths and passion in life. I wanted to learn more about becoming even more productive, increasing self-efficacy, and helping others in similar situations. I researched the theories and models out there, but none of them really served me well or answered the burning questions I had to my full satisfaction.

If we want to see improvements in our life every day, if we are willing to put all our intellect, knowledge, and our heart into the game, we need to make sure that we are served best with the right challenge-skills balance. Everybody deserves a fair chance to develop personally, live a healthy life outside of business hours, and play an important role in their network of family and friends. I decided to join and help shape this new world and developed a new formula that incorporates both: improving performance for a successful, thriving professional life and developing yourself to live a more balanced, healthier, and happier life. NOWING® was born.

Initially I started to implement the exercises and tools in my own life and asked friends and family members to volunteer to try out one or another activity. Then I conducted an international research project as part of my thesis paper to test the key parameters of the NOWING® Formula—and it worked well. Soon I received amazing feedback from the first participants in my program, and they gave me confidence that NOWING® should be available to a bigger audience. I wanted to make sure that as many individuals as possible could avoid the ten years I went through before knowing what works best, fastest, and is sustainable for today's digital lifestyle.

At the heart of NOWING® is the understanding that everything we do is not about yesterday or about tomorrow, but about today, about being here now. This is the basic stance that we need to train ourselves in if we want to be successful over a long period of time. The six elements of NOWING® help to answer the most critical questions on the way to high performance and greater well-being:

- *How to get the fundamentals right: your social backbone, physical environment, practices and rituals, and your drive for connection and creative expression.*

- *How to find your path to clarity, getting your priorities straight, avoiding distraction, and mastering self-organization.*

- *How to focus on achieving a flow state with the right mix of challenges and skills needed to perform at high levels in the digital industry.*

- *How to collaborate, work, persuade, and influence others to achieve your desired goals in a way that serves the creation of innovative ideas.*

- *How to treat and feed your body and brain along the four dimensions of motion, food, presence, and cognition.*

- *How to gain clarity, refocusing on your life's purpose and your true passion in order to think big and bold and without fear.*

Don't wait and waste the ten years it took me to find out the answers to all these questions. Get ready for the new world here and now, and master your personal NOWING®.

OUR PLAYGROUND IS THE DIGITAL INDUSTRY

Talking about individual performance and health, especially for the next-generation workforce, entrepreneurs, and up-and-coming talent in all industries is one thing. But understanding the environment is always first. How does the playground look where young talents are learning their first lessons and are building their network and drafting plans for their professional career and their private life? The impact our environment has on us has been proven in so many studies—whether this is your private four walls, place of work, desktop, or your favorite living room corner—whatever you make out of the space you live and work in reflects directly on your performance, well-being, and motivation. So let's have a look at the big-picture environment we currently see around us.

The only constant is change—this catchy phrase is more true right now than ever before. In the middle of the digital transformation, disruption and unpredictable turbulence, complexity, dynamics, and competition are the themes that all of us need to deal with. Being part of this digital transformation is vital for companies of all sizes—small- and medium-size companies as well as large corporations. Start-ups apply new business models, and by doing so they disrupt entire industries. Many players that have dominated the market in the past decades with innovative, high-quality products and services need to be very careful not to miss this fast digital train that's about to depart the train station. Some say it has already started to move but has not yet gained full speed.

This digital playground is characterized by daily technological innovation that has had and will have the power to radically change entire cultures and mentalities—just as Gutenberg's printing press did centuries ago. The same is true for the Internet as the key driver in the current digital transformation: it has the enormous power to change, influence, connect, and uncover like no industrial invention ever before. The Internet is built on meritocracy, where leaders are defined on the basis of individual ability or achievement. This means that living in this era is less about title, expensive business school degrees, status of your family, or marketing budget for your new campaign. None of the typical status symbols or definitions is of importance anymore; they are not critical for success. Hierarchies will not be defined up front. No. It is the number of followers one can generate that defines the ability to lead and to share a message.

The concept of sharing will also dominate our future—in business and in our private lives. Sharing our couch and our home with strangers via online booking tools and sharing our car with others are only two examples of this new trend, a new value in our future society and economy—a trend that will also affect the next generation's attitude about how to deal with resources, by the way. There is much more concern for ethical, sustainable, and fair handling among all citizens of this planet than we have ever seen in any generation before. When I say "we share," it means more "we don't need to possess" but behave resourcefully. It means we optimize the use of our materials, our places, and our own internal resources, our own bodies.

To paint a picture of this digital playground from a customer's perspective only means creating a drawing where we find ourselves in a fully seamless and individualized world where we say with pride, "Nouns are dead—long live the verbs." Understanding and acknowledging the power of the consumer and prioritizing consumer satisfaction in terms of online and real time is significant, not to say essential for survival. In this picture it is less about owning a car (noun) but more about the "ability to move from point A to point B" (moving = verb). It will be less about buying a home (noun) but more about enjoying space to live in (verb). The power of personalization will replace mass products and impersonal experiences, and the capabilities of technical devices—in professional as well as private life—will take over routine tasks, which will not bother us in the future. Your fridge will—most likely—not drive to the grocery store in the near future to get more yogurt and butter, but for sure your fridge will be able to automatically put a note into your calendar at the right moment to order yogurt and butter, because there is only enough for one more breakfast and one more dinner. All this, paired with self-service, robotics, and new technologies, will automate many of our daily tasks.

The bases for these developments in the digital world, for individual as well as for corporate success in the future, are the magic four: openness, interconnectedness, participation, and agility. If you are afraid of any of them, you will be in a tough position in the future. But if you welcome them and see them as triggers to go beyond and above what has worked in the past and bring yourself, your team, your organization, and your network to the next level, you will find yourself at the tip of the spear.

The trouble many organizations face, however, is their lack of understanding about where to start and what to do first during these challenging digital times. It is even worse than that: the majority of leadership teams have only limited—if any—understanding of what digital transformation, industry 4.0, connected anything, and the shared economy is all about and what these mean for them and their team, not to mention no idea of how to measure and evaluate the digital maturity of their own organization.

Digital maturity has a lot to do with analyzing which digital trends there are in the market. Are there any potential threats due to new technologies? Which (new) channels are relevant, and what is the digital service and value proposition a company offers? The most fundamental question, however, is this: Which skill set, competencies, and environment are needed within the organization and on an individual employee level to make the digital change happen and to jump on the train rather than getting hit by it?

SKILL SET FOR LEADING
THE DIGITAL GAME

The digital transformation is taking place in times of great economic and social change. Most companies will not have an option to join the game or not. They and their employees are simply forced to play by the new rules of these digital times. But there is something these organizations can influence, and this is crucial for mastering the transition: it is preparing their leadership to navigate the entire organization through this disruptive sea.

From a management perspective this means that it is still necessary, even in the digital industry, to take good care of the classical management tasks:

Define Goals and Strategies: Managers need to define the direction that the market in which the organization exists, with all its entities, products, and services, is heading within a given time frame.

Organize Collaboration: Managers are responsible for creating the environment so that their teams can complete their tasks—even complex, international projects—and co-operate in the best possible way real-time, hassle-free, and technologically supported.

Ensure Communication: Managers have a duty to communicate in such a way that all the necessary information is understood and delivered to the point of interest. Each individual needs to be informed about the essentials relevant for performing their tasks, and mechanisms for providing feedback must be in place. The decades of information-hoarding are gone; sharing with a high level of sensitivity when it comes to data security is not the future but the present.

Apply Management Tools: Managers need to ensure that all members of the organization know what to do, which general framework to consider, how to motivate and, if needed, how to deal with misbehavior.

Foster Innovation: Managers have the duty to ensure the existence of their organization in the future, which means they need to deal with the skill development of their workforce, promote creativity and innovative capacity in each individual, and provide the basis for creating new products and services.

For all those managerial tasks there is a plethora of applicable tools and methods available. Picking the right one and applying it the right way will remain as challenging in the future as it was in the past. But what makes management in the digital world even more difficult is that all those tools and techniques are not enough anymore. It is the order of the day to "pimp" the classical management tools with elements from the digital space. Let's take the classical task of "defining goals and strategies," for example. This should not be done in a static, sequential way once a year at a strategy meeting but should rather be adjusted and developed on the run in order to react to current trends and sudden changes in the market. It's like planning a new sunscreen campaign for July, which is, in terms of the season, a smart thing to do. But if it is raining for a week, you postpone that campaign despite all the planning (and financial/marketing) effort that has been put into this project for July. Rather, do your promotion with three weeks' delay but good weather, and don't stick to your initial marketing promotion plan.

Management in the digital industry will be more about dealing with dynamics and allowing change to happen. It will be like trying the "Columbus spirit" when he started his voyage to discover India. Preparing an organization for the economic challenges of the twenty-first century is a bit like discovering virgin soil. It is

- *less about control but more about unfolding;*
- *less about guidelines but more about serving leaders;*
- *less about patronizing but more about appreciating;*
- *less about subordination but more about participation;*
- *less about "work-to-rule" but more about going beyond oneself; and*
- *less about planning everything but more about discovering step by step.*

There is a rather new yet interesting and promising approach to master all these challenges in our fast-changing economy and make any organization ready for great flexibility. It is called "Holocracy"—a system for complete self-organization that should help even established organizations overcome old and partly outdated operating models. Many define Holocracy as the third alternative to traditional hierarchy and flat-management approaches because it brings structure and discipline to a peer-to-peer workplace. But above all these new approaches and systems, there is one key success factor that will tip the scales when it comes to managing a successful organization in the digital world, that is, human maturity at key positions in an organization.

So what are the top leadership skills and tasks that one should prepare for in order to play a vital role in any future organization? First of all, it is about understanding that decisions are no longer a privilege (or obligation?) of top management but will be decentralized in the future. It won't be the head of global marketing that decides when and where to launch the new product but the marketing experts on the ground, closest to the market and the customer, those who know the best local weather in which to promote sunscreen. Then there is the aspect of real-time information that allows for but also requires fast decisions instead of lengthy information processing, business casing, and scenario analysis. Third, prospective digital leaders will say it is their core task to inspire rather than to manage, and they need to be prepared for and work with a new definition of diversity: teams consisting of people with multicultural backgrounds, collaborating in real life and virtually, paired with intelligent machines and robots—that's the new team of 2020. Last but not least, leadership in the digital industry needs to understand the big importance of value creation over process control, and there must be less responding to market dynamics but more innovative initiatives for different markets.

All this requires new approaches to successfully train and develop ourselves and the next generation of urgently needed talents. But first one needs to understand who those key players, those "digerati" or digital-savvy millennial talents, are. What distinguishes them from the previous generations and which strengths do those digital talents have that can help shape the future in a positive way?

THE PLAYERS IN THE GAME ARE Y TALENTS

Despite all the technological innovations taking place, we need to keep in mind that there is a human factor that plays a vital role in the digital industry. We can automate processes, we can have robots as new team members, and we can work with smart, connected, shared devices that tell us what we want before we even know it. But there is no organization—to date or in the future—that can operate without any human beings at all. The true success factor for companies in the twenty-first century will be human maturity at the right key positions of an organization. So the questions of the day are—Who are the main actors in this disruptive digital game? What distinguishes these up-and-coming talents of generation Y from their parents and grandparents?

The makeup of the global workforce is in the middle of a massive change, where today half of the employees in the world are considered millennials or generation Y—born between 1980 and 1997. Millennials are the children of generation X and the large group of baby boomers, the majority of whom is about to retire. This Y generation has been strongly influenced by the impact of the Internet on our daily activities: work and life are strongly interwoven, personal opinions are expressed directly and openly, and their new personal lifestyle shapes how entire societies think, act, and collaborate. Understanding how these most important players of the future workforce tick and what makes them perform and live a purposeful life is essential for a successful digital revolution in any industry.

One could fill a bookshelf with articles and studies that have been published on this markedly different generation of millennials. Yes, there are differences that are worth remembering, and yes, there are still a lot of values, interests, strengths, weaknesses, and desires that remain the same as in previous generations. Being a millennial myself, I once was asked in a plenary discussion to introduce myself as "the typical gen Y / millennial." Here is the transcript of my answer:

I (as a millennial) favor the entrepreneurial spirit, a high level of independence, and yes, I'm digitally savvy with strong objections to micromanagement. I love empowerment, I love challenge, and I love excitement, thus I have a more unorthodox approach to career management that does not parallel traditional paths. I view traditional hierarchies and authorities skeptically, but I bring an impressive portfolio of academic credentials and skills to the workplace. What do I want in return for putting those skills into action? I aim for fast-track promotions, nice salary raises to fuel my nonprofessional areas of interest/hobbies, flexible work arrangements to combine professional and family life, and yes, there needs to be a reason, a bigger purpose, and, of course, fun in whatever I am supposed to be doing. I want meaningful work that adds value, and I appreciate constant feedback and recognition. I am also very impatient, so don't you dare promise a distant pay raise or promotion—this will not get my attention.

It is typical for us millennials to find different and rapidly changing workplaces over the course of our careers. What will remain constant from one job to the next, however, is that we have certain expectations of ourselves, our supervisors, and the organizations we work for.

To start with ourselves first, generation Y wants to learn technical or core skills in their areas of expertise because they fully understand how necessary those skills are in a digital environment. We are also extremely interested in learning skills focused on self-management and personal productivity as well as leadership skills, which are needed to solve current management challenges. All this should come with some sprinkles of industry or functional know-how and should be presented in a creative, innovative form or environment.

Our expectations toward the company we work for include the development of skills needed for the future, paired with ongoing professional coaching as we have been used to since our childhood days: whether it was our parents, neighbors, family members, or friends, there was always a good "coach" ready for a good conversation geared toward finding the best solutions. We also want a company with strong values and individualized offerings and benefit packages: from B as benefits to S as salary and W as working time. Organizations ready to gain and retain Y talents have to allow for—but not require—blending work with private life, and a clear career path must be presented.

Last but not least, the question remains of what millennials expect from supervisors or "the boss"—a term Ys would never use because of their dislike of hierarchy. The "boss" is supposed to help navigate the career journey and provide constant, timely, and thorough feedback. This person should not only help guide but also coach and mentor on an informal basis and act as a sponsor in formal development initiatives. And, by the way, he or she should not have an issue with flexible work arrangements.

In a nutshell one could say that millennials are not willing to trust "old-school" schemes and sources such as preachy old advisors or traditional career tracks. Given that generation Y will make up more than 50 percent of the global workforce by 2020, any company succeeding in attracting and working with millennials sits on a gold mine for future business success. Gen Y'ers are ambitious for thriving careers and charged lives, thus they will see progress in their professional lives, will see income growth, and see an increased possibility to pay for premium services. So if an organization has not yet disappointed them and manages to be attractive to them as customers and employees, chances are high that these organizations are well prepared for future success.

Understanding what drives this critical generation Y is one thing. But what are the skills in general that we should look for, regardless of being a millennial or part of an older generation? What should we train mainly young talents in for playing a vital, challenging, satisfying, and important role in the digital era? To perform well, there are four golden capabilities one should master—and hopefully more educational institutions as well as individual students will start emphasizing them:

- *problem-solving skills*
- *leadership skills*
- *communication skills*
- *technology skills*

Those are considered essential skills at the beginning of the twenty-first century from executives around the world. In addition, we will see future leaders and next-generation talents in digital-savvy organizations with a thriving career who are ready to experiment, curious and willing to learn, and above all, ready to fail—fail fast, fail forward, and most importantly, learn from their failures for future endeavors. Digital talents are considered highly adaptable to new situations and possess a great degree of judgment and the power to decide. They are very eager to collaborate, to find out how something works rather than following task descriptions, rules, and guidelines blindly. And there is one more attribute that distinguishes these highly successful future colleagues: they fully understand and live true to delivering value.

This Internet-savvy generation Y, with its focus on speed, openness, transparency, and global reach, is contrary to current management representatives who value quality, safety, privacy, and personal relationships. This changed mind-set, paired with a changed approach and a changed set of values and beliefs, will allow for taking on new perspectives and even generating new job descriptions such as a "generation integrator" or "digital disruption specialist."

Whether an organization can then motivate all generations to join forces in creating innovative and successful solutions remains another differentiating yet critical factor for high performance of any business in the future.

GETTING MOTIVATED
FOR THE DIGITAL GAME

The motivation rules of the industrial game in the last decades can be summarized as a "carrot-and-stick approach." This worked well for routine, unchallenging, and highly controlled tasks. The process is straightforward and lateral thinking is not necessary, thus benefits and incentives can provide a small motivational boost without side effects. But the environment has changed dramatically, as have jobs in the digital industry. They are more complex, more interesting, and more self-directed...and this is where the carrot-and-stick approach does not work anymore. So what are the new rules of the game? What works and makes us achieve the best performance in these challenging days of the digital transformation?

Thanks to different disciplines from brain research to behavioral sciences, from sociology to psychology, from medicine to organizational development, we possess today more knowledge and scientifically proven evidence on how to achieve the best performance than ever before. We understand today what we do, why we do things, what makes us do things better, and what we can do to increase and decrease our performance in any aspect of life. If we only applied what we knew. That's the real pity of today: there are all the answers on managing our performance in the best possible way, but in terms of what we apply, what we teach our students, what we incorporate into our organizations, and what we implement in our daily life, it is like climbing Mount Everest in a bikini. No wonder we experience so much trouble with frequently falling down and being hurt, getting off track, not making it to full speed, and never experiencing the greatness of reaching the top.

Thanks to the new values and success criteria embraced by generation Y, there is finally a chance now at the digital entrance to the twenty-first century to implement what scientists have been trying to tell us for decades:

- **Motivation:** *People have a strong intrinsic motivation to perform a task, especially where there is a great degree of autonomy.*
- **Community:** *A good community will solve any problem, especially complex ones, faster than individual firefighters.*
- **Purpose:** *Humans are much more interested in serving a purpose than doing tasks for monetary rewards only.*

To understand what is needed for the best performance, one has to analyze what drives us, what motivates us to perform at the top level, to reach our best. Psychologists and management practitioners came up with different theories about and approaches to human motivation: Maslow approached it from a psychological realm, with motivation revolving around human needs and motives. Management scholars like Herzberg focused their theories around incentives and inducement frameworks. And Gestalt psychologists focus on perception being the only determinant of behavior. It is not only the intensity of the motivation that counts but also the quality or type of motivation an individual experiences. Qualitative or controlled motivation occurs when external forces affect an individual's behavior, whereas the much more appreciated autonomous or intrinsic motivation occurs when individuals feel that the reason for their motivation comes from within, making them act autonomously, according to their will, as they have internalized the reason for acting.

Psychologist Mihaly Csikszentmihalyi can be described as one of the pioneers and founding fathers of analyzing and understanding top performance and happiness. He observed high performers in different disciplines—sports, science, economics—and realized that they are capable of achieving excellent performance over a long period of time without getting exhausted. He called this state *flow*—a state of concentration on the activity at hand and the situation, in which nothing else matters. This flow state is an optimal state of intrinsic motivation, in which the person is fully immersed in what he or she is doing. In order to make a flowlike state and "full happiness" possible, three main parameters must be met:

- **Autonomy**: *I can decide for myself which task I perform when, how, and with whom.*
- **Competence**: *I have (or have access to) the necessary skills, resources, and environment needed to perform a task.*
- **Relatedness**: *I understand why I am doing this task, what this task means for the bigger cause, and I experience a feeling of security and belonging.*

To make the best performance possible in the digital industry, we need to make sure that these three key parameters for allowing flow to happen are understood by each individual and the organization as such. Even more importantly, we change the organizational setting in a way that allows individuals to act autonomously, easily acquire and access the needed competencies, and understand the purpose of the work they do.

For some organizations this sounds like a difficult, tedious task, whereas others consider this the basics of a good management practice. Wherever you and your team are on this scale, let's highlight the most important elements allowing for great performance, especially in today's digital era:

Clarifying goals: The mission of the organization must be clear to everybody, including line managers and each individual subordinate. Make every possible effort to keep the lines of communication open, allowing plenty of time for talking and exchanging ideas. In this context it becomes even more important that leadership takes on the responsibility of "chief inspirer," drawing a picture of the ultimate goal that looks so promising and irresistible that all employees are fully engaged and eager to follow and create outcomes.

Allowing for trial and error: People learn and perform best if they are given a large amount of autonomy to test and try things out, to learn by doing it themselves in their own style rather than following their supervisor's guidance. Making great innovations possible—the ultimate necessity for any business if it should exist in the next five to ten years—requires a new culture in which the one who tries and fails is not damned but celebrated as a hero and admired for the experience and the courage to stand up again and give it another try.

Immediate feedback: To know what's next it is necessary to understand where you are, how much closer you are to the goal, or what worked well/did not work well in the past. Thus, the best information to receive—and to give—is immediate feedback. This could come from people around you or your work/work-related systems directly, which could provide feedback about the status of your performance. Feedback should also come regarding your own personal standard and how you are performing according to your own goals and core values.

Balance challenges and skills: The use of each individual's skills and the entire human capacity of a person should be matched with an adequate level of challenge. The balance of these two never remains stable for a long time but requires ongoing adjustment in order to keep up the performance. No doubt the winners will be the ones who constantly build and work on their skills as they take on more and bigger challenges over time.

Concentration over monkey mind: For many, stress is not the result of too much hard work but of too much switching attention, handling constant interruptions, and dealing with ever-changing requirements. Thus, people should be given more control, access to the right skills and tools to reach the requested objective, and the trust that they will make the best choices.

One can ask now if fulfilling those requirements is an organization's duty or the responsibility of each individual employee. The answer is simple: it's both parties' task to ensure that work at least close to a flow state is possible. Why? Because it will be the individual who enjoys work much more and who can remain healthy while achieving great results, and it is the organization that will benefit if its workforce outpaces competitors as a result of its high level of performance.

Five

Introduction to
NOWING®

H umans are today at the edge of their comfort zone. Real-
time, 24-7 use of technology, connected everything,
and extremely fast-paced virtual environments—all of this results in increased performance pressure on up-and-coming
talents. The lines between business and private are more and
more blurred, limiting the opportunities for individuals to relax, recharge, and recover. On top of this is the impact of de-
mographics, with a significantly reduced number of potential
talents for future leadership roles and an aging workforce not
at all familiar or comfortable with digital fancy. The most innovative and profitable companies today and in the future realize that high performance of individuals is only possible when
you also engage in improving health and well-being.

It is time for a new era of helping to learn rather than
teaching. Forget about all the lengthy, multiday trainings,
theory-based-seminars, and annual leadership development

programs you are used to. Since everybody has a different starting point, a different challenge and also the need for a different action plan, these generalized trainings and courses do only so much: they teach general things to an individual audience, with the results that you walk away with many "nice-to-knows" but with almost no "can-apply-for-myself-right-away" customized action plan.

The NOWING® Formula is different compared to many of the established methods and approaches out there from the predigital era. I am passionate about providing you with a unique, tailor-made plan to achieve your personal goals and create your individual path to success, at your pace and with the challenges along your way—nothing generalized. Everything absolutely individualized.

With this book you will first learn the elements of NOWING® in detail, which means, you will be able to start today to make the first improvements to your performance and your health and you will see the first results kicking in within a few days if you follow the activities. I invite you to get out of your comfy chair, get active and get moving toward your personal vision and your real goals, the ones that make you feel really satisfied and cause a big smile to cross your face. I believe you can do this and I am passionate about helping young, talented professionals like you to get the best they can and to train them to the top level they deserve. I truly hope you don't waste another ten years like I did before you start but that you instead give it a try today, right now.

BASED ON THE FINDINGS OF AN INTERNATIONAL STUDY

In 2014 we conducted an international study[1] to understand what drives the generation Y especially as the critical demographic group of up-and-coming talents in the digital industry. How can they be motivated to be fully here and now in their early adulthood in order to increase performance and improve their well-being? The results of this cross-sectional survey showed that the level of happiness and well-being is strongly influenced by generation Y's internal motivation and level of mindfulness. Individuals of this age group can efficiently master their motivation with the use of selected approaches like the NOWING® Formula.

The term "NOWING®" is a combination of six essential elements for mastering a digital lifestyle, and it is about being here and now, which matters in life and makes the difference between the good and best performing individuals. It can be described as a proven process for working with more clarity, satisfaction, motivation, energy, and presence as well as a much lower stress level. Subsequently, your mental balance, your well-being, and your overall health will improve.

Going on this transformational journey with the NOWING® Formula will cause you to raise the bar for your personal performance and your resilience so you can consistently achieve above the norm.

---

1   Michaela Lindinger, "Millenial Motivation to NOWING® - How can Millenials develop motivations to be fully present in their early adulthood?" (master's thesis, University of East London, 2014), http://hdl.handle.net/10552/3911.

At the heart of this approach is the understanding that everything we do is not about yesterday or about tomorrow but about today, about here and now. This refers to the importance of mindfulness as uncovered in my 2014 study. Nevertheless, mastering mindfulness doesn't solve all the challenges of the digital era. So there is a set of six core elements making up the term "NOWING®":

(1) **NEST:** This element is all about getting the fundamentals right, in other words, your social backbone, your physical environment, your practices and rituals, your drive for connection and creative expression.

(2) **ORGANIZE:** This element covers the path to clarity by getting your priorities straight, avoiding distraction by focusing your attention better, and mastering disorganization by doing the important things first.

(3) **WORK:** This element focuses on achieving a flow state with the right mix of challenges and skills needed to perform at high levels in the digital industry, proactively making bold decisions and living true to yourself.

(4) **INTERACT:** This element is about how you collaborate, work, and influence others to achieve your desired objectives in a way that serves the creation of innovative ideas.

(5) **NURTURE:** This element covers how we should treat and feed our bodies and our brains, and it runs along

the four dimensions of motion, food, presence, and cognition.

(6) **GOAL:** This element helps you to gain clarity, refocusing on your life's purpose and your true passion in order to think big and bold, without fear.

Over the next chapters you will experience a deep dive into each of these six core elements, along with useful exercises that you can apply right away. Before you start, however, be aware: the NOWING® Formula might have an impact on you, your career, your daily life, your well-being, and your overall agenda. If you are ready for a positive change, continue reading.

SCORING HIGH IN THIS GAME

Before we get started, let me share with you some basics that will have a tremendous impact on your NOWING® journey to greater performance and better health. Once you are aware of the playground and you understand the players, the question remains how you can score high in this game, in achieving what this powerful formula makes possible. If you give it a try and stick to those simple but important basics, your personal success on this journey is almost guaranteed.

Be patient with yourself: I know this is not what you want to hear when you are all excited about getting started. But I have joined many of my clients from all different backgrounds on their personal journeys and the reason I always get results for them is very simple: I know from a psychological and

Michaela Lindinger

learning theory perspective what it takes to change things, and I know—despite all the difficulties—that being patient, taking your time, and spending enough time on critical steps is the number-one success factor in this journey. Being patient and having persistence will move the needle for you eventually and will make the difference that you are looking for.

Write it down: The human brain is capable of doing a lot more than we currently know and definitely more than we currently make use of. Nevertheless, I want to force you to get yourself a journal dedicated to this personal journey, in which you will make notes of all your ideas—the ones that come along while you read, while you complete the exercises, maybe while you are on the way to work the next morning and recap what you read in one of the chapters the night before. So please, get out there, find a nice-looking journal that is dedicated to this personal NOWING® journey, and fill it up. Yes, fill it up with all the great ideas, thoughts, and questions that come to your mind.

Practice common sense: When I grew up in my small, very traditional Austrian village, there was a lot made of learning the common sense dos and don'ts of society. Nowadays I work with so many brilliantly educated people who seem to lack this significant learning. Nobody told them the basics; there were no parents or grandparents who had a serious desire to help them make something of their lives and teach the right behavior. So common sense seems to be very difficult for some people. And that's a real pity because common sense is not common practice anymore. Keep in mind that what you will learn in this book is less about theory and more about practical, applicable tools based on world-class theory. And it is about putting common sense into practice.

Get good company: As human beings we are not born to live all by ourselves, and especially in times of significant change, when you lay the foundation for your future lifestyle, for the dream that you are going to achieve, it is essential that you have good company. So please reach out to a person you enjoy working with, somebody who is visionary and capable of asking you the right questions that will help you a step further. Trust me, this transformation will work much better if you have some good company willing to put his or her own agenda aside—someone who wants to help you find your purpose and dream, who is a real supporter in guiding you through tough decision processes, a person who accompanies you in complex change situations and who is willing to help you find your way through upcoming challenges. In any significant personal change journey, I personally find it most rewarding to have someone who is competent and willing to help me reflect on my own behavior. I hope you already have someone in mind who will be your personal support. If you are struggling to find a professional and competent partner, book a free initial strategy call with me personally. Go to www.braininspa.com and pick a date and time that is convenient for you. This offer is only available for a limited time, and I make only a limited number of slots available each month. Grab your slot before you have to wait too long and make sure you check out all the bonus material on www.braininspa.com. There is really no easier way to get started than with the help of a professional NOWING® master and some useful work sheets and templates. Find out what additional benefits you purchased with this book.

There is a valid question I hear from executives and young talents alike: How come we live in a performance-based society with health-care costs going beyond affordability and schools or universities that don't teach us how best to prepare ourselves for healthy survival in this digital fish tank? Let's assume for a moment that you study business with a major in marketing; then of course you will learn all different kinds of theories of consumer influence models, and, of course, the instructors will teach you with cases and practical examples how to transfer this knowledge to the real world. But where they hardly ever teach theory and where they *never* teach practice is in the space of personal development, in creating and achieving your dreams and your perfect lifestyle. Schools don't consider it their duty to show you ways to make a great career and still have a valuable private life with time for family, friends, and sports, thus living a happy, resilient life as a citizen in the digital society. So why are all these essential lessons and insights not taught in any postgraduate program? Why? Because they don't show up on the curriculum! Because some of the best universities out there haven't yet figured out how to keep up with the speed and pace that the new digital world requires. They are way behind what the big global industry players out there require from their best people, their best future leaders, and their digital talents.

I am sure you don't want to wait for them to update the curriculum in 20xx, but rather you want to prepare yourself best for the most challenging, most rewarding, and most exciting career and life out there. And if you want to do things differently, if you want things to change, there are only two ways for that to happen: either something new comes into your life (a new tool, a new idea, a new plan), or something new within you comes up (a new fire or belief within yourself causes the change).

Now you are well prepared for scoring high, and hopefully you can call the NOWING® Formula this "new something" that came into your life and caused change to happen. Let's have a look at the elements of the NOWING® Formula in more detail.

Six

Element 1: NEST

The term "NEST" should be taken as a synonym for getting your fundamentals and your groundwork right. It is like building a new house: you carefully pick the land, have good reasoning why you are doing it at all, and know which outcome you expect and who you select to build and design your new home. The same applies to getting the fundamentals right for your life as a healthy and high-performing individual: you need to get your purpose clear and strategically investigate your social backbone. It is essential that your environment is a reflection of you and that there are clear rituals and practices in place. For those truly valued individuals in our society who take on the strenuous task of raising the next generation—also called parents—there is an additional note in terms of building a nest.

GET YOUR PURPOSE CLEAR
It is a daunting task to finally figure it out: What is the reason for us being here? Most of us don't even bother thinking

about a good reason, a unique aim, or intent why we are here. And yet, on our final day, all of us struggle, and we feel we didn't have enough time or didn't make use of the time given in the best possible way to serve our personal mission. Whatever your personal answer is to the question of why you are here, make sure you are happy and you focus each day on working toward that mission, toward that personal intention, so when your final day arrives, you can say with pride that you know why you were here and, even more important, that you are happy and satisfied with what you have achieved.

It is essential to have an answer to why you are doing what you are doing, because it helps you to focus, to guide almost all your thoughts, words, and actions. But this is common sense that's not commonly practiced, simply because we get caught up in all our day-to-day activities. Imagine it is like the piece of land you buy that you carefully pick and choose before you build your house and your garden on top of it, where you then raise your children and spend time with your friends. Your personal mission statement is like the basis for building this nest, your environment to reflect, to recharge, and to envision the future.

One way to define your personal mission statement is to ask yourself the short but powerful question "Why am I here?" A good start to answer this big question is by completing the sentence "I am here because.../ The reason / The aim for me being here is..." Try to think of different aspects of your life—relationships, work, money, and you.

- **Relationships:** *include those with your spouse/lover, children, parents, friends, and so on.*
- **Work:** *covers your current and future work ambitions. What/how is it that you want to spend your days? With which content, which format, which lifestyle, which product/service?*
- **Money:** *should obviously cover your financial future.*
- **"You":** *covers aspects of body, mind, spirit, and interests.*

Those big questions that sum up your personal mission statement can't be completed on a nice evening with a good glass of red wine. It will take some time if you haven't asked these questions at all till now. And no, there is no personal mission statement developed once that is valid forever. You have accomplished a lot if you can finally write down the three to five key sentences that answer the question of why you are here and what you would like to achieve as of today. And when things change in your life, your mission statement also changes. Think of any company that started out as a small enterprise and grew bigger and bigger with international expansion. Its mission statement has no doubt been adjusted several times over the course of the company's growth to reflect the new status quo.

Unlike in some companies where mission statements become "developed-once-but-never-really-took-it-for-real" things, your personal mission statement must be your compass. Make sure you place it somewhere visible in your life, whether this is the bathroom mirror, your top desk drawer, or inside your closet that you open every day to get new socks. Wherever it is, make sure you are reminded of where you want to go in these four areas—relationships, work, money, and you.

Still struggling? Here is a more brutal but very powerful tool in finding out what should go into your mission statement: imagine x years from now, you are invited to attend your own funeral. You have the rare opportunity to hear what your family, friends, and colleagues say about you and your life, about your accomplishments, about your character, about you working and living with them. What is it that you would like to hear? Which type of person would you like to be in their memories? What character traits of yours and the way you influenced their lives should remain in their minds?

If I'd only known this before...yes, afterward we are always smarter than before. But we also have the unique ability to choose up front where we want to go before regretting that we have taken the wrong path all life long and didn't arrive where we wanted to get. To begin with the end in mind should help you develop a clear understanding of your destination. It should help you paint the picture you would like to see at the end before you go on the journey. Knowing the final destination helps you better understand where you are now and which steps will serve you best to progress in the right, desired direction. To think about your personal "Why?" in different dimensions—family, job, hobby, friends, and so on—will not only help you to align your resources, but it motivates you, because whatever you are doing is worth doing (for the "why" behind it). It gets your focus clear, and having a clear and well-thought-out "Why?" is the best decision-making criterion you can ask for.

PROACTIVELY DESIGN YOUR SOCIAL BACKBONE

One of the most critical elements when building your nest is your social backbone. People with real, active social relationships, like friends and family, are happier compared to isolated single fighters and also more psychologically stable. They suffer less from illness, more resistant to depression, and stand up faster when they fall down. The foundation for this starts in our early childhood. If we are blessed to experience supporting, loving, caring parents, we are more likely to develop a healthy self-confidence, and we are able to anchor this as a real asset for the rest of our life. It gives us this unique yet essential feeling that we have someone next to us or behind us, a helping hand we can always grasp that is always there for us when we need one. Those social networks are almost like a life preserver that helps us swim in "rough sea" phases of our life. And this is not only valid during childhood but also at any age during our adult life. For children it is primarily the parents and the close family who is important; later, the safety net grows bigger and includes friends, colleagues, teammates in sports clubs, and so forth.

In theory all this sounds perfectly right, almost self-evident, but reality shows the opposite. Lack of time, busy schedules, too much work, lack of energy, caught in the "must-dos" are just a few reasons many of us have no time for their social network. For some the social network is even reduced to colleagues at work because this is where they spent most of their time. If these people lose their job, they lose their entire social backbone along with their job—and that's troublesome.

Living in the social media age, there is a new dimension to the social backbone that needs careful consideration. Some years ago nobody would ask how many friends you have, not to mention how many people follow you. With the rise of social networks, people are crazy about increasing their number of "friends" and "followers." They sometimes overlook the fact that this is not to be counted in the same way as real friends. Our online social friends and networks are certainly interested in us, our topics, and our life, but they won't serve as a safety net when we really need them.

So what are the main benefits of having a real-life social network made up of friends, family members, colleagues, and so on? One benefit is that you can turn to them for advice, and they will help you when you need answers or when you can't figure out how something works. Another benefit of your real network is that you can experience and enjoy things together. Whether this is going on a hike, preparing a meal, or celebrating the best quarterly financial results—doing all this alone is by far not the same as doing this with at least one person who is close to you.

If you have started to think about the similarities and differences between your real and your virtual friends by now, you are on the right track. Why not take some time to start painting your very own personal "social network map"? It can help you gain more clarity and identify people who are good for you and with whom you don't interact with enough. Here's how it goes:

———————

* *Write your name in the center of a piece of paper.*
* *Identify the various networks, social and otherwise, in your life: family, friends, clubs (sports clubs, music clubs, etc.), colleagues, neighbors, church/spiritual groups, and so on.*
* *Write the names of each of these groups around your name and draw a line linking your name with each of these social networks.*
* *Now list the people who belong to each of these groups. If you have three siblings named Susan, John, and Victory, then those three names should be placed in your "family" group*
* *Write the name of the person you are closest to in each group right next to your name in the middle; the person or people you barely see and interact with should be located farther from your name.*

———————

Have you identified your status quo with your existing social network? Now ask yourself the following for each group:

———————

* *How do I define a happy and close relationship within this group?*
* *Who are the people I love spending time with and whose presence reflects positively on me? Draw a little smiley face next to these names.*
* *Who is missing from each network? Add those people's names in blue.*
* *Who should be closer to my name / farther away from my name? Highlight those who should be closer in yellow and those who should be farther away in red.*
* *What could I do to deepen my relationships with certain individuals?*

We are always surprised when we see how little attention we pay to the types of people we interact, engage, and spend precious time with. More and more studies are proving that the quality of our close friends and relationships is one of the most significant factors in determining our overall emotion, resilience, stability, and success. So be careful with whom you interact daily because these people have a direct impact on your level of satisfaction and your perspective on life. And then there are people we consider toxic. Yes, "toxic" is a harsh word, but that's the truth in this context: these people will poison your life and not help you reach the level you dream of. There is no better day than today to gradually move them out to the far edge of the map, interacting with them only the bare minimum, even if they belong to the groups "friends" or "family." There is the saying that you can't choose your family, but you can choose who in the family to interact with and how often. And if there are family members who are toxic but you "need to" see them each Sunday or every other Saturday for a brunch, you always have the chance to change the schedule to once a month—or even less frequent. The choice is yours.

Knowing this, take another look at your social backbone picture. Identify one or another action item in terms of whose name needs to come closer to yours. Maybe there are individuals in each group whose names were written close to the center, but, as a matter of fact, these people are not good for you?

Your social backbone is a highly individual thing, and there is no right or wrong in terms of how many groups you identified, how many people you have in each group, and how many are written close to your name. Nevertheless, there is a rule of thumb as to what we consider healthy and helpful for feeling happy and satisfied in life. Every person should have a handful of five to ten "close" friends who physically see one another at least once a month (all of them or just one of them) and who speak to one another on average once a week. These close friends are people who know you really well, encourage you to go after your dreams, challenge you to become a better person each day, and, last but not least, are simply fun to be around.

And what if you found out that you need to (or want to) intensify contact with selected individuals? Here are a few

ideas that require small effort but create big impact for getting started:

Real Network. Mark your calendar at least once a week
to reach out to your real social network, or maybe even block
some time each week in your calendar that is dedicated to
one of your social network groups.

Birthdays. Mark individual birthdays in your calendar—
and give them at least a call or drop them a note on their
birthday.

Little gifts. Surprise them with a little gift every once
in a while. This could be bringing something from the bak-
ery, sending their favorite tea, inviting them to come over for
breakfast or dinner, or just send a picture of a beautiful day or
a flower from your garden to brighten their day.

Toxic people. Watch out for the "toxic" people who
just make you feel bad and unwanted and who criticize you.
Sometimes this can be very close family members, and it
might take time to realize that their company is not good
for you. That doesn't mean you don't see them ever again.
Just reduce the time you dedicate to them, and you will be
amazed how much better you feel if you slowly but surely
get rid of all the "toxic people" in your life.

Authenticity. Be honest and present when you meet your
social backbone: don't just pretend. Say when you are happy,
and don't hide feelings when something is bothering you.
Real, true members of your social backbone will be open as
well and won't misuse your honesty. Also make sure you are
present and pay attention to them. The time you spend with

them should be time with just them—no phone calls when you have lunch with your friends, no e-mails when you promised your child you'd play cards, and don't let your buddies wait half an hour at the tennis court because you had to finish something at work. Give your real, true social backbone the attention and presence they deserve—and they will return it multiple times.

Investing in your social backbone always pays off because it helps you get clarity on your current network, and it should support you in identifying people who will help you move closer to having a more charged, successful, and happy life. There is one more thing we can learn from happy married couples or great teachers: you get what you look for. Unfortunately, people are trained from their early school days to look out for mistakes and failure. Criticism and "shit storms" have become really popular. The news is filled with "attack here," "lying individual over there," "scandal in company A." The view through these highly negative lenses doesn't make it easy to search for the positive, to believe in the power of "positive projection." But it still exists. Having an optimistic view in your constant search for the good and interesting in every person and situation will help you find the interesting and good aspects of individuals and situations in your life.

MAKE YOUR ENVIRONMENT "YOU-ISH"

The people we consider as our social backbone, who we interact with, are only half of the process of building our perfect nest. The environment we live and work in is equally important and can have a significant impact—positive as well as negative—on our overall performance and well-being. The influence of light, fresh air, high-quality state-of-the-art equipment, taking breaks, and the opportunity to engage socially cannot be stressed enough when it comes to pushing our individual performance to its peak. Your workplace should be more than merely functional; however, it should also be attractive and reflect your personality. How comfortable do you feel with the style, color, and appearance of your personal work area? While very few people actually have the chance to design or redesign their office or work space according to personal preferences, you can definitely make the most of what you have. Make sure ergonomics comes first and ensure that your desk/screen/chair positions are correct. Then take care of proper lighting and fresh air as well as keeping your space properly organized and your papers filed—if you need paper at all.

Really beautiful places make us feel better than ugly, messy, dark ones, right? Imagine a stroll on the beach, a hike in the mountains, reading a good book under a palm tree, whereby positive emotions result and replace negative thoughts. The same is true for your home, your private four walls. Walking into your home should feel like entering the most peaceful place, where you are free to be completely yourself, where you can relax, recharge, have fun, and find new ways to live a purposeful life.

The good news is that we can generate these positive emotions anywhere. We simply need to define "free zones," for example, in our house or apartment, which can simply be a corner where you have your favorite chair, a lovely painting, and your best reading table. Pick a spot within your private four walls where you can hide yourself for ten to fifteen minutes, and enjoy this time as if you were on a little island in the middle of the hectic daily-life sea. It is best if you decorate this place with pieces that bring up good memories—whether it is the coffee mug your best friend gave you years ago; the first picture of your dog when he was still a puppy; some sand from the beach you enjoyed so much during your last vacation, or your magic golf club that helped you get your first hole in one. Make sure you use this free zone at least once a day, and leave all business outside this magic place; just go there to relax and enjoy, to bring back memories of great moments.

Remember when you were a child and you had your favorite spot to hide, where nobody could find you? Make this free zone such a spot, where you are safe, not to be disturbed, and just surrounded by good emotions. There are people who have used their free zones with such passion that after a while it was enough simply to walk by or to look at this corner of their home or garden and it put a smile on their face.

The environment—whether at home, at work, or at school—does affect us to a significant extent, so it is important to decorate the place where we live in a way that makes us feel comfortable, energized, and happy, as well as to make sure the places we spend our precious time reflects our need for creative expression. These places need to be a real reflection of you:

----

* *How much do you see of "you" within your private four walls? Is your home customized to suit you, and does it really reflect who you are? Do you feel good in your home because it reflects "your style"?*
* *How unique and customized is your work space? Is there an individual space that you have designed "your way"? Think beyond your desk—your clothing, the style of your e-mails, your signature, and your meeting style.*
* *How much do you customize your leisure activity to "you"? Do you read the magazines you really prefer to read, and do you go after the hobbies you want to experience rather than those somebody told you to do?*

Designing your environment in a way that I call "you-ish" means adding your personal color and flavor to your surroundings. It is about leaving a unique footprint, your personal contributions to any situation, to any project, to any relationship, and certainly to any space you live in. The more "you-ishness" you bring to your space, the happier you will be as you experience your daily challenges. There is nothing tricky about improving your individual expression in one or all areas of life. Decide right now where you need more "you"—at your desk, in your living room, with your spouse or your best friend, when going for leisure activity—and decide right now what you will change. Right now. Make it happen, and add something more "you." Right now.

CHECK YOUR PRACTICES AND RITUALS
Now that we have taken care of our personal mission statement and discussed the importance of our real social backbone and the environment on our overall performance, we should bring a bit of structure into life.

When you have little children you learn really fast that the more routine they experience during their days the more relaxed they are. Why? Because they simply know what's happening, when to expect what, and, since lunch always follows breakfast, there is no chance to miss it. What works for little children does a very good job for adults as well. We as humans are programmed not only to appreciate change, which we need to grow, develop, and climb to the next level, but we also need the safety of routines and recurring rituals that make us feel grounded, feel at home in our center ring, and feel secure.

It is essential that we make ourselves aware of the rituals we currently have and that we enjoy because of the structure and the predictability they provide. Once you think about your rituals, you can go from detail to high level—from brushing your teeth to planning summer vacation each March. With a little structure in identifying your routines and habits, you might also uncover areas in which you are not yet so structured and could give yourself a little hand with developing more defined rituals.

Having clearly defined practices for a daily, weekly, monthly, and yearly schedule helps to start out. There are rituals and habits that belong to your professional life, to people around you (family, children, colleagues, etc.), to your personal learning and development, to your health and well-being, and, last but not least, to your finances. For all of these areas of your life you should have a plan and established practices in place that help you each day get a step closer to your ultimate goal.

For each of these aspects, try to complete the following sentence: "In the area of X (for example, health), I could set up the following practices or routines to find some more structure and improvement on a daily basis/weekly basis…" An example could be "In the area of health, I can set up the following practice to get into better shape: on a daily basis, walk to the office instead of taking the bus; on a weekly basis, go jogging at least twice; on a monthly basis, have two to three swimming sessions."

Creating this plan for a monthly time span or maybe an entire year is essential. But don't make the mistake of sticking to a plan if your reality has changed. Rather, adjust your initial plans frequently and do a little validity testing at least on a monthly basis.

The method I use to revise my personal plans in the different areas of my life is what I call my "Friday Sprint Session." Every Friday evening I take thirty minutes and "sprint" through all my achievements from the week and think about what's necessary to focus on next week. The basis for these sprint sessions is, of course, my overall plan for the key projects I am working on. The same is done on a monthly basis on the last day of each month (it is a one-hour meeting marked in my calendar), when I try to look at a more strategic level if I am "on track" for the right challenges or if something new appeared that needs to be taken care of and that deserves priority over other projects.

There are people who love these kinds of exercises, and they jump right into doing their personal "sprint session," analyzing their current rituals and practices. And then there are others who seem stuck because they never thought of adding more structure to their daily life. For them it is enough of a challenge to have Christmas decorations up on time or to manage getting through their mornings without major hiccups. In case you are closer to the last type, here are some starting points for good practices that are worth considering for a potentially new schedule:

---

* *Start your day by asking yourself, "What will I achieve today?" and finish your day with the same question: "What did I achieve today?" Before you get out of bed and before you fall asleep are good times.*
* *Schedule "you" time. We are so busy that we overlook how much we need some time just for ourselves. Make sure at least*

one or two times a day you have fifteen to twenty minutes just for you—no e-mails, no calls, no cooking, no reading, nothing other than relaxing and quiet time.

* *Time for breakfast, lunch away from your desk, and dinner with a person you value and appreciate—at least one must happen every day; best-case scenario—all of them happen in one day.*

* *A piece of learning each week: a good book, time to read your favorite magazine, study time on a subject you are curious about.*

————

Admitting that I belong to the partly overorganized species, I have to say that my life is filled with structure and rituals that help me stay organized despite all the flexibility my lifestyle requires. I have, for example, fixed days and times for grocery shopping, and up till then everybody in my family fills the on-line grocery app shopping list with items they need. I love to have pajama breakfasts with my family on Sundays and read my favorite magazine. I start my days with a little morning exercise to focus and set the objective for the day, and I close my days being thankful for what I have experienced and accomplished, asking all my other guardian angels to help me make tomorrow a bit better than today. I am also hooked on rituals related to the four seasons or to holidays. Whether this is baking my own Christmas cookies in December or decorating my house for Easter, spring, and during Advent, it helps my family and me to have orientation, structure, and a feeling of safety despite the ever-changing daily challenges.

A NOTE FOR WORKING PARENTS

For some of us there is one more aspect of building our nest—it is about our role of being a parent while still having professional ambitions.

Nobody thinks of this beforehand, but once you have your own family and children, you might ask yourself, *How the hell should I combine doing what I love with being where I like to be?* It is like walking a tightrope: the path to mastery is very, very small, and there is no one-size-fits-all solution. We all know the topics around child care and how important it is to find one that fits your specific needs—if there is one available at all. Having worked with a large number of parental returners and with working mothers of different backgrounds, I have my personal hit list of three things that help to master my individual version of keeping my career and children parallel, instead of in a sequence. I am not saying that these three approaches solve all my problems when it comes to walking that tightrope. But considering them could help you at least become a bit more stable in your daily performance:

Make it a strategic approach to find the right work scenario that fits your requirements. I have always advised my friends and clients to start creating their top ten criteria list—what is it that you absolutely need to have so you can enjoy doing your job? Because without real excitement and fun, you will quickly face the question "Why the hell do I deal with all this?" In addition, you should also create your list of absolute no-gos. One of my personal no-gos is a job where I have to be at the office before 8:00 a.m. Need a little helping hand to get started with your list? Let me give you some ideas: start time in the morning, type of work, team/leadership role, average hours per week, after-work duties, home-office possibilities, content, access to training, use of remote tools, career development, distances between work and home, child care, company mind-set about working parents, type of clients/providers you work with, age of colleagues/team members, office location, office interior/design, and so on.

Good enough is good enough: Many parents, especially women, get very frustrated about not being able to keep up to prechild levels when it comes to personal perfectionism. Nails are not done daily in the color matching your outfit; the home front-door flower decoration does not match each season of the year anymore. The laundry is not done during the week, so you need to spend some time on the weekend. This list could probably go on and on forever. I am sure as you read this, you can add with the blink of an eye at least three things that bother you because they have changed, and you are not really on top of them anymore. The reason is simple. You have more roles to play in the same twenty-four hours of a day. The worst thing you can do now is to keep up the struggle and try to maintain your prefamily perfectionism or routine. That time was a part of your past, and now things are different. That doesn't mean it is better or worse; it is just different. The beauty is that in everything we face, we can find something good. So instead of getting frustrated about what is not as it used to be anymore, find the things you like. Spend the time you used to do your nails playing a card game with your children; instead of studying cookbooks for a Friday night four-course menu, cook something simple and healthy together with your family. Instead of struggling through your closet every morning, trying to find things that match and that are not in the laundry, invest once in a style guide (book or personal), and create a closet where each item has more than one match.

Separate, separate, separate: Whatever role you are currently in—your work-related role, your role as a parent, your role as a family and home CEO—be present, stay focused, and don't mix roles. When you drop off your child at kindergarten or at your best friend's place, trust that they will take good care of your little one, and don't call every thirty minutes to see if things are OK. When you are at work, focus on the stuff you need to get done, and don't let yourself get distracted by thinking about your child, your home, or your laundry. When you are in the role of the family manager, don't take business-related calls—it just causes stress and trouble; believe me. There is nothing worse than your little toddler screaming while you are trying to convince your new big-deal client to sign the project agreement. Make sure you take on only one role at a time, and stay focused on this one before you switch to the next. A friend of mine is a successful actress and manages to balance her work and private life really well. She once told me that any good actor has to go offstage to switch clothes before playing another character. The same is true for you with different roles—go offstage for at least a few minutes in your mind, change character, and be fully present again in the next role. Going offstage doesn't have to last long; it could be another two or three minutes in the car before you hit the front door, listening to a good song on the bus on your commute home, or changing clothes when you switch from business to private settings.

CHECKPOINT ON NEST

Below you will find the key questions and thoughts related to this chapter. This "fill-in-the-blanks" exercise should help you get started. If you need more templates or work sheets to help you through each chapter of this book and to get the most benefits out of the NOWING® Formula, visit www.brai-ninspa.com and download your free workbook.

———————

* *My personal mission statement reduced to five key sentences is...*

_____

_____

_____

_____

_____

* *My social network map shows that these are the people I want to intensify contact with...by doing...*

_____

_____

_____

_____

_____

_____

* *My social network map shows that these are toxic people I currently interact with too often...so I will change my level of interaction with them by doing...*

  _____

  _____

  _____

  _____

  _____

  _____

* *To make my work environment more "you-ish," I will do the following three things...*

  _____

  _____

  _____

  _____

  _____

  _____

* *To make my home environment more "you-ish," I will do the following three things...*

  _____

  _____

  _____

  _____

  _____

  _____

*   *The practice/ritual that I will start doing/emphasizing is...*

_____

_____

_____

_____

_____

_____

*   *As a working mom/dad, I will stop/start/continue doing...*

_____

_____

_____

_____

_____

_____

———————

Seven

Element 2:
ORGANIZE

For some of us, talking about organizing means dealing with time management—the art of using your time in the best possible way. Others claim this is absolute nonsense because you cannot manage time; it always goes by at the same speed: twenty-four hours each day, seven days a week, 365 days a year. That's only one reason why time management is not the solution to the problem of getting more organization in our lives. Better we learn to manage the way we work; how we plan, organize, and prioritize; and how we direct all our daily efforts.

Most people do find a little mental chaos when they look inside and struggle with the three most common problems from not having clarity and an organized life. First they find **confusion**, which is created by them not setting clear priorities, having no clear path ahead. Then they discover **distraction**, all those thousand little things that keep their attention away from the stuff that really matters. And last but not least, they often find overall **disorganization**, which causes them to think in a disorderly manner, with no productive results. In order to gain clarity and to solve these most pressing issues, there are three obvious yet sometimes difficult steps to take:

- *Solve confusion by getting your priorities straight.*
- *Solve distraction by focusing your attention better.*
- *Solve disorganization by doing the important things first and getting rid of the irrelevant to-dos.*

If you want to get ahead faster, you need to change how you do things today as well as what you focus on. It really comes down to strengthening your ability to produce more of the right stuff in the same amount of time. Focus on the really important things, and you will efficiently produce more daily progress, which does make a difference.

IDENTIFYING PRIORITIES

There is this feeling some people call "being overwhelmed." It makes them unsure about where to start because there are a trillion things requiring their attention. Others call it "being off-balance" because something feels just not right, not balanced at all. And then there are those who keep repeating what nobody can hear anymore: "I am so stressed. I don't even know where to start." Whatever you call it, it is a feeling that seems to be very prominent these days, and it is a sign that you are not living by your priorities. Maybe you live on autopilot and take care of whatever others require you to do, what you are supposed to do, or what your family or your boss requested that you do. Isn't it time to get your balance back, to be your own master and complete those to-dos that bring you closer to your desired goals? So it is critical that you define which priorities you have for your life, specifically right now, for this exact moment in your life.

Before getting started with a framework for evaluating all the chances and opportunities that are presented to you and acting based on your priorities, there is an underlying idea you should understand first. Therefore, let me briefly introduce you to one of the most inspiring individuals I know—Viktor Frankl.

He was a psychiatrist and because he was Jewish he was imprisoned in the death camps of the Nazis, where he experienced things that were too horrible to even imagine. His parents, his brother, and his wife all died in the camps, and Frankl himself suffered enormous torture and agony, never knowing from one moment to the next if he would be sent to the oven or if he would be lucky again to survive the day. It was during these agonizing days when he became aware of what would later be quoted a million times: **between stimulus and response, *you* have the freedom to choose**. Frankl realized that whatever happened to him (the stimulus) and how he responded to this stimulus, he himself (and nobody else) had the freedom to choose his response.

Transferring this learning of Viktor Frankl to our daily struggle, it means that at every given moment you have a chance to choose: you can say yes or no, do it or don't; you can go left or right. Most importantly, once you have identified your vision and your key priorities in life, you should say no to everything that comes your way that tries to distract you or that takes away time from your priorities.

Assuming you have a clear vision of where you are going with your life and you have defined your goals, then you can judge which activities help you go in the right direction, and you have a complete overview of all the projects—private and professional—that are going on in your life right now. In assessing whether something presented to you is a priority and should get your time and attention, ask yourself only two simple questions:

---

* ***Is this really my subject?*** *Understand if you have the ownership for this topic and if it is important for you / your goal. Identify if this has a real impact in your life and if this is relevant for your bigger purpose.*
* ***Is there a real demand with a real deadline and a required action behind this?*** *Try to understand what happens if you didn't do it – would something really bad happen?*

If one or both of these questions is answered with NO, there is no required action from you, so either disregard the task/

topic presented to you or put it on your "maybe of interest someday" list. Answering both of these questions with YES means that you need to deal with the subject, allowing for your time and attention. Here is the secret of true productivity masters: it is the three-minute-rule. If the required action derived from this request takes less than three minutes of your time and you can do it right away, get it done. If the task needs more than three minutes, delegate it and make sure it shows up on your "waiting for" list. You can also put a date on the task as to when you will schedule time in your calendar to work on it—for example, a presentation or a conceptual paper that you need to write in which you need more time. I learned from some true productivity masters that they tend to schedule their typical meetings—like talking to a colleague on subject X, calling a client on topic Y, and so on—for fifteen minutes instead of the commonly used thirty minutes. Without question, this allows you to fit many more potential discussions or meetings into your calendar and helps participants to focus because fifteen minutes moves pretty fast. Last but not least, you could place this task that takes more than three minutes and is relevant to you on your "next action items" list, on which you collect all the to-dos, maybe structured by topic or project. This "next action items" list is your number-one go-to place when it comes to defining your day or your week.

AVOID DISTRACTIONS
Gaining clarity does also mean getting a handle on all the thousand little things that keep distracting you, not only on

a daily basis but even on an hourly one. We start task A, and then the phone rings; we jump over to topic B that the caller wants to discuss. Then an e-mail comes in from our boss replying to a request we made two days ago—we are curious to read it. And oops! We have no clue where we actually stopped and what it was that we wanted to do with the initial task A.

We know there are some jobs and some types of distractions that are relevant and essential and need to be dealt with immediately, like your child coming home bleeding from the playground or when a patient in the emergency room stops breathing. But those types of real emergencies are the exception—distractions that are OK and important. Most of the time, distractions are far less important and don't justify all current tasks being stopped immediately.

The human brain is less likely to perform at optimum levels by 20–40 percent if tasks are done in parallel instead of sequentially. Other studies even say that a short distraction of two or three minutes means that it takes ten to fifteen minutes to get back into the initial task. In short, every distraction is a pure waste of time and focus. We also know now that every shift from task A to interrupting task B also means increasing the failure rate. So what is a good path toward working with more focus and attention, going toward more clarity and less distraction?

In your calendar. If it is not in your calendar, it is a "dead task." So whatever it is that you are trying to structure and schedule, unless it finds its way into your calendar with dedicated time blocks to deal with it, it will never be done. Also, make sure you have completion dates for the final task as well as for subtasks. The same is true if you want to learn something or acquire a new skill. Define what you want to achieve by when and how you will get it done and on which days.

Time blocks. Structure your work/productive time in blocks of twenty to thirty minutes. Dedicate those time blocks to one topic each, and work without distraction on what needs to be done. A very powerful technique for structuring your work in time blocks is the Pomodoro® technique: you set a timer for twenty-five minutes; then you give your undivided attention to subject A. Then you have a five-minute break before you go into the next Pomodoro session of twenty-five minutes. After four Pomodoros, you deserve a bigger break of fifteen to twenty minutes. It is all about working *with* your time, not *against* it. It helps avoid burnout and trains you to focus and get rid of distractions, subsequently helping you fight procrastination and foster happy, successful days.

Stopping a task. Never stop just anywhere in a specific task; always try to finish at a point that at least closes a chapter of the task. Just imagine going grocery shopping; you've just started your tour of the store when your best friend calls and ask you to go for quick coffee close to the store. You would not just leave the cart where you are, not pay for your already collected items, and run over to see your friend. You would rather finish at least the groceries you need most for the weekend, check out, and maybe come back a few days later and pick up the remaining items on your list.

Interruptions. Whenever something interrupts your current task, decide immediately if it is a real emergency (ask yourself, "Will somebody die if I don't deal with this now?"). Deal with only real emergencies; ignore the rest and maybe make a note so you don't forget to set time aside for dealing with the issue.

Troublemakers. If there are certain people who are always troublemakers in terms of interrupting you, make sure you talk to them as soon as possible. Don't assume they do it on purpose, but tell them that their constant interruptions keep you from working productively. Discuss with them how you would like them to approach you or when it is a good time to discuss new topics.

Take notes. Take notes of all the ideas that come to your mind while doing task A but that are relevant for tasks B or C. Writing down these ideas should be done in a structured way and most likely with the help of the right tools—this could be Excel spreadsheets, calendar solutions, brainstorming tools, or online collaboration systems. Taking notes also allows your mind to refocus its full attention on the task at hand, knowing that nothing is lost because you just documented the idea.

Distraction these days is not always related to other people interrupting our work. It is often e-mail, status updates, or phone calls that make us lose our focus and attention. Being online 24-7-365 is not what makes you more productive. On the other hand, there are real online addicts who can't stay away from their Twitter or Facebook accounts, their mobile phones, or their mailbox for more than thirty minutes. Either way is not helpful for your productivity. In order to use all the different media wisely and to de-stress your work life, follow these steps:

Free is free: Make sure you define your free time as really free time from any media used for business purposes. This is especially true for weekends and vacation time. While we have many organizations and many supervisors requesting that their employees be available anytime at least via phone or text message, there is a countermovement taking place right now in which companies agree—all the way to the top level—that there should be no e-mails or phone calls outside of regular office hours. Some organizations these days even shut down mail servers on purpose so nothing gets through. Whatever type of professional surroundings you work in, make sure there are clear lines for you personally that you don't allow others to cross. Weekends, evenings after work, and vacation days are such red lines where you should allow nobody to bother you.

Not within reach: Define times when you cannot be reached. This means that you don't pick up the phone just because it rings in the middle of an important meeting. When you are at lunch, for example, or having a coffee with a friend or colleague, ignore incoming e-mails and phone calls and instead focus your attention on the ongoing conversation. Yes, I am absolutely serious: you can ignore a ringing phone, because there is voice mail that can take messages, and yes, it is absolutely fine to call back when you have the next time block scheduled for returning calls.

Communicate your OOO: There is always the option for out-of-office (OOO) notes or status messages in your online tools, so you can let your audience, team members, and clients know that you are currently not available—whether you are on vacation, at a two-day workshop, or in a lengthy interview. What you should do, however, is provide an option to leave a message for you, and make sure you follow up. When do you make time for this? Well, this is again part of you setting your priorities and determining when you would like to make room in your calendar for answering messages.

FIRST THINGS FIRST

There are way too many books and magazines out there on how to manage your day in the best possible way and solve disorganization, many with similar approaches and many with contradictory ideas. The good thing, however, is that it's not at all difficult to define what's first in your days, weeks, and spare time. Once managed, it helps you in a way that you feel charged and happy with what you have achieved. You only need to understand a few rules and apply them with consistency.

Let me invite you to a little experiment, and afterward you will look at self-management from a different perspective because you only have to remember one picture. Imagine a vase that you normally use for flowers, and that vase represents your twenty-four-hour day. Now I ask you to fill this vase with tennis balls, as many as you can. When you have placed the last ball, I ask you if the vase is full now. Yes? No? Well, most of us would say yes because no more tennis balls fit into this vase. What if I then gave you a basket full of little marbles—well, they easily fill out the vase and use the space in between the tennis balls. And then I give you a bottle of water and you pour that into the vase and the water even fills up the space between the marbles.

Now, what does this tell you about organizing yourself and managing your time? Why should you remember this picture of the vase filled with tennis balls, marbles, and water? The answer is very simple: the number-one secret of self-management is focusing on the important, essential things *first* and then dealing with the rest. Taking our little vase experiment, the tennis balls represent the big topics, your big goals, the things that matter in your life, the topics that make the difference for you and that bring you a step closer to your goal. It is essential that you place and schedule them first so they get the space, time, and attention they deserve. Then the second-tier duties and tasks can make use of the room in between, and if you still have time for more small stuff, like water, you can add this on top and fill up your day—but you could also skip the water and leave some air in between so you are flexible and have enough time for breaks in between activities.

This picture of the vase should help you when it comes to setting priorities and keeping the focus on the "tennis balls" during a day, over a week, or over the course of an entire year. But how do I know what my personal "tennis balls" are? This is a question I hear many times and the "lifetime pie" could be of help for you in answering this question:

———————

* Draw a circle to represent a pie that represents an average day or week.
* List all the elements of your life that require time, for example, family, job, sleep, eating, commuting, sports, friends, hobbies, travel, household duties, education, religion/spirituality, and so on.
* Calculate based on sixteen hours a day (twenty-four hours minus an average of eight hours for sleeping) how much time you spend on each of the areas of your life in percentages.
* Split your painted pie into elements—as you would cut a pie into pieces—and the size of each piece represents the time spent in percentage on this area of life. So, for example, if you spend 25 percent of your lifetime in an average week working, then you should indicate that one quarter of your pie is reserved for work.
* Take a careful look at your pie. How much time do you spend on which activities and life areas? Is this how you would like it to be? Where do you think you spend too much / too little time? Are there areas that you would like to be smaller/bigger? Are the biggest pieces of this pie serving your personal mission, helping you answer the whys behind your life?
* Indicate with a plus (+) or a minus (–) each piece of the pie that should get bigger (+) or smaller (–). Obviously, all the pieces that get a plus are the areas where your "tennis balls" belong.
* Write a list of three things you can start doing today to change the first piece to make it bigger or smaller.

WORKING ON YOUR DAILY FOCUS

Chances are high that after doing this lifetime pie exercise you will realize that there are too many pieces that need attention. Some pieces need to get smaller; others you want to grow bigger. And the more you try to work on all of them, the more you start forgetting or overlooking things. Scientists have proven over and over again that on average we are capable of dealing with seven, plus or minus two, things at once. Whenever we try to manage more than seven key projects, tasks, topics, and so forth, we run the risk of losing control or overlooking or forgetting parts. For great, extraordinary performance we should focus on fewer, on seven projects that we deal with at once. There are outstanding individuals like scientists, artists, and athletes who manage to achieve amazing results because of their focus on fewer—but therefore with 100 percent attention. Sometimes this means purposefully leaving things untouched, not taken care of, and outsourced to somebody else. So your focus, your effort, and your time is fully concentrated on your key seven. Make sure you pick a maximum of seven pieces from your pie to put your focus on, let's say for the next month or quarter, and once those seven are taken care of, you are ready for the next set of seven.

Managing all your projects and focus tasks requires a good organization of the twenty-four hours of each day. It is critical to do this in a way that makes you not only satisfied but also shows that you have accomplished the necessary steps that bring you closer to your desired goal. Many people struggle with starting their day, then they get all confused and get trapped in micromanaging before they go to bed much too late, having had a busy, exhausting day but not having accomplished one single thing that would bring them a step closer to their objective in any area of their life. In case you have had such days in the past—most of us have had more than one of those days, unfortunately. Here is a super-powerful tool that helps you to stay very focused if you apply it consistently: a daily focus sheet.

---

* *Each morning when you start your workday, write on a piece of paper your top three or four projects that are currently the focus of your attention. Those key projects go on top of your daily focus sheet.*
* *Now each project gets one next-step action item (from a potential list of many next steps that you defined for this project). These next-action items are the tasks that you need to work on today. You will do nothing else until you finish them and have potentially room for more. Sometimes it is three or four next-action items for one project that we can complete in a day, and this means we push this project closer to completion than we planned for on that day: fine. But focus only on the one next-action item for your most important projects, and you will get away from the "there-is-so-much-to-do" feeling and closer to the*

"wow-I-did-move-this-project-in-the-right-direction-today"
feeling. The latter is better; believe me.
* *Below your key projects, make a "waiting for" list—this is a*
  list of people you need input/feedback from and also a list of
  people you owe feedback/information to.
* *Complete your focus sheet with a maximum of seven bullets*
  for little to-dos of the day, like errands you need to run, a pick-
  up you have to make, and so on.

———————

Create your daily focus sheet in a way that you find personally appealing. I have mine created on a single sheet of yellow paper so I can always find it; it is friendly and positive to look at, and it hardly ever gets into the pile of other white pieces of paper. You can download a free copy of my personal daily focus sheet at www.braininspa.com.

When you start to master your self-organization, there is one more secret that will boost your daily performance: get back the power of your mornings. The first hour of your day is—I would almost say—"holy" and should not be wasted on any social media, in your inbox, or doing household chores. Be aware that your first practices of the day can help you create a phenomenal frame for the day. When you wake up, you might want to spend one or two minutes with a little energizer exercise and remind yourself out loud of your overall life vision and your dream life. You should explicitly set your intentions for the day: What is it that I would like to accomplish today? What is it that I am look-ing forward to? What is it that I would like to complete/start today? Then make sure you hydrate your body again after a whole night of sleep with a cup of your favorite tea or simply water, because we lose a few hundred milliliters of water during sleep. Whether you take a long shower in the morning, go for a walk with the dog, or postpone your workout till late evening is up to you. But what you should neither skip nor postpone is enjoying a healthy breakfast, ideally with the company of your family members. Do not ever check your inbox in the first hour of the day. Your mail-box is only the storage place for other people's to-dos and should not reflect on or direct your thoughts early in the morning. The first hour of the morning is sacred time for you to set up success, so set up your day your way.

CONSIDER YOUR CLOCK WITHIN

Organizing ourselves and our days in an efficient way can be even further improved by arranging the tasks in the best pos-sible sequence. There is a field of biology that examines bio-logical rhythms in living organisms, including human beings, which is called chronobiology. The most important rhythm studied is the circadian rhythm, a twenty-four-hour cycle shown by physiological processes in all organisms.

Looking at the typical working time of a twenty-four-hour day, we can identify three main phases: before noon from eight to twelve, noon between twelve and two, and afternoon between two and seven. Let's examine how we should structure our day according to our chronobiological clock.

From when we get up in the morning until nine we are at the peak of dexterity, which means that any task in need of precise finger movement should be scheduled then. If we then move on to the tenth, eleventh, and twelfth hours of the day, we are in the time of the best possible creativity. So any task or project that requires you to be creative, to come up with something new, to allow for innovative concepts and ideas should be scheduled before lunch. Especially complex or complicated tasks that require you to focus, to think through, and to use your full cognitive capabilities are best done during these hours. Depending on the country you live in, anywhere between noon and 2:00 p.m. is the typical lunchtime. The same is true for our body's internal clock: during this time frame, we are programmed to rest and to recharge. If you have the chance you should even consider taking a little time off, maybe even a short power nap around 2:00 p.m., or apply some relaxation or meditation technique. Refrain from squeezing in important phone calls, difficult conversations, or tricky project tasks right before your lunch break—chances are high that they won't work out to your full satisfaction. After our "lunch low," our performance capability goes up again until about 5:00 p.m., when we experience the second performance high of the day—the first one was between 10:00 a.m. and 12:00 p.m. At around 5:00 p.m.

we are working really fast and our muscular strength is at its peak, which allows us to do the most effective workout during this time of day. After six or seven in the evening, the body's overall performance slowly but surely goes down, preparing the organism for a good night's sleep.

Chronobiology doesn't say that all organisms work the same, but it should give you an indication. It will hopefully inspire you to review your current schedule and compare this to the chronobiological schedule. Maybe there is an answer for why certain things you are trying to accomplish at a specific time of day don't work out as expected, whereas others just thrive.

CHECKPOINT ON ORGANIZE

Below you will find the key questions and thoughts related to this chapter, and don't forget to download your free workbook at www.braininspa.com.

----

* *I understand the sentence "Between stimulus and response I have the freedom to choose" and I will apply it by doing...*

_____

_____

_____

_____

_____

_____

* *Every task presented to me will be scrutinized with the following two questions: 1) Is this really my subject/topic? 2) Is there a real demand/urgency/deadline?*

_____

_____

_____

_____

_____

_____

* *Every task I consider relevant for my overall objective finds a space in my calendar.*

_____

_____

_____

_____

_____

_____

Whenever possible I structure my day in small slices of twenty to thirty minutes with short breaks in between, so today will look like this:...

_____

_____

_____

_____

_____

_____

* *I will not stop a task anywhere but at a defined stopping point.*

_____

_____

_____

_____

_____

_____

*   *All the ideas that come to my mind while completing one task will be noted in a journal/tool so they are not lost but don't distract me in the middle of my work. The journal/tool I will use is...*

_____

_____

_____

_____

_____

_____

*   *Every week I have defined free time when I am not available to any business inquiries. These free time slots are...*

_____

_____

_____

_____

_____

_____

*   *Drawing my lifetime pie shows me that...*

_____

_____

_____

_____

_____

_____

* *I have my vase with tennis balls (the topics are...), marbles (the topics are...), and water (the topics are...)*

  _____

  _____

  _____

  _____

  _____

  _____

* *My daily focus sheet looks like this...*

  _____

  _____

  _____

  _____

  _____

* *I will start to structure my daily schedule according to my chronobiological clock tomorrow in the following way...*

  _____

  _____

  _____

  _____

  _____

  _____

Eight

Element 3: WORK

Whatever you do for a living, the way you work, the way you make decisions and get ready for new challenges, the way you speak up for yourself and your ideas—that makes a difference. Being more successful and achieving higher performance means you are willing to take the risk, you are up for a challenge, and demonstrate bold actions and willingness to acquire all the competencies and skills needed. You show courage and make your way despite potential criticism or others trying to hold you back. The tough get going when the going gets tough, said one of my great mentors.

If one doesn't enjoy one's job—whatever it is—one can't be very good at it, right? Having fun with what you do is important, but you cannot just say, "I am working on this for x hours and then I will have fun"—that simply doesn't work. So what is it that we have to look for in our tasks that have the ability to improve our life in the long run?

As mentioned earlier, one of the key elements for great performance is the right balance of skills and challenges—the better the performance should be, the more you must progress and learn more skills, getting to the next level of complexity. According to Mihaly Csikszentmihalyi, each person has control over how many challenges he or she wants to deal with, and there are eight different combinations of challenges and skills that affect health and high performance—apathy, boredom, relaxation, worry, anxiety, arousal, control, and flow.

The more skilled you feel to perform a certain task, the more your overall happiness will improve. The more challenges are presented to you—at an adequate level—the more focused and concentrated you will be. The best-case scenario is when challenges and skills are above average, allowing you to enjoy a real state of flow. If this is not the case, you are either low on challenges axis, with your skills being bored, feeling "only" relaxed, or you face challenges but lack the skills, which causes you to worry, get stressed, or at worst, feel pure anxiety. The more your levels of challenge and skills are in sync, the more you feel happy, in control, and focused.

The quality of our performance and subsequently the progress toward our overall life goals, our desired lifestyle, largely depends on our ability to improve the skills needed to master the challenges we face today:

- *how to solve problems;*
- *how to lead in a digital environment;*

- *how to master our resilience;*
- *how to communicate and interact successfully; and*
- *how to do nothing despite the plethora of temptations, just being present in the here and now*

All these skills are essential, and it is less a question of which one is more important than the others and more a question of how we can improve all five of them simultaneously. As mentioned earlier, the key driver for success in the digital industry won't be technology but healthy, innovative human performance at critical positions. Thus, the skill of communication is covered in a separate NOWING® chapter, "INTERACT," and mindfulness is part of "NURTURE." This leaves three skills that belong to the chapter "WORK": problem solving, leading digitally, and mastering resilience. Outstanding performance is only possible if those skills are adequately matched and balanced with the challenges presented.

SOLVING PROBLEMS

Generally speaking, problem-solving skills allow us to adjust our behavior and responses to any changing situation in an effective way. Without a doubt, these digitally disruptive times teach us a lesson in how critical it will be for future success and high performance to quickly analyze what's going on, to overcome blocks in finding a solution, and to apply techniques for creating a practicable action plan.

In order to find the appropriate answer to your problem, start by asking the following key questions first:

---

* *What are the key facts and which relevant information do you have available regarding the given situation?*
* *Why is there a need for change? Where does the complication come from?*
* *What is the key question that you are trying to answer in order to solve your problem?*
* *How can you break down the issue at hand into smaller pieces and logically take apart the large problem so it can be analyzed and solved?*

You can't work out a good solution without answering those four questions first. The key to effective problem solving is dealing with the real problem, not its symptoms. Find out what is really going on, what the real problem is, not one of the symptoms. Challenge yourself to look at the issue presented from different angles, and don't commit yourself too early, risking taking the "wrong path" to a solution. Considering any issue from different perspectives can mean looking at it through the eyes of the following:

---

* **Client:** *who is the client, and how does this issue affect him or her?*
* **Stakeholder:** *who is involved in the situation?*
* **Process:** *which systems/entities/units are affected?*
* **Bird:** *what is the bigger picture, the world view from a bird's perspective?*
* **Environment:** *which constraints affect the potential solution?*

———

There are many problem-solving techniques out there, and one could fill an entire book by itself. The point here is to encourage you to improve your problem-solving skills and to learn and master at least some of the tools and techniques out there and apply them when needed. Sometimes we are dealing with problems that are straightforward. Fine. Solution finding is less difficult and does not worry us too much. But then we have those complex issues, those for which you don't know where to start in terms of taking all relevant aspects into consideration for developing a good solution. Mostly, visualization helps to make sense of this messy cloud. You can use a simple cause-effect diagram or create a flow chart or a swim-lane diagram to help you spell out your issue or your issue tree.

Did you solve your challenges in the past with a pre-defined tool, or have you created your own, personal problem-solving approach like a framework you apply for any complex challenge? The better the approach you have, the more successful you—and subsequently your team—will be in the future when confronted with new challenges of the digital era. Working successfully in the digital industry does not mean building a reputation as someone who shies away from problems, delegates them to subordinates, or pushes others hard to find a solution. No. Great problem-solving skills manifest in your ability to see challenges as a gift, your ability to handle tough situations in a wise, positive, and results-oriented way. One of my great mentors used to say, "If God wants to hand you a present, he wraps it as a problem: the bigger the problem, the bigger the present."

LEADING DIGITAL

If you have ever had the chance to be in a leadership position in your professional or even in your private life, you are probably very familiar with all the challenges that leaders face. When we talk about great leaders, most of us think of individuals with extraordinary skills, decades of experience, who are well educated by great business schools and executive programs—individuals with phenomenal character strengths, with innovative visions for themselves, their teams, and their company. We think of individuals who are masters in motivating not only themselves but also others and who manage a team in a truly inspiring way.

To me this sounds almost impossible. When I started out in my first leadership role, I thought that half of these attributes were essential to becoming and being a good leader.

First I was excited about finally making it into a leadership position, getting the promotion. But then I got a bit frustrated and almost discouraged because I did not know where to start, how to lead and inspire my team, how to be visionary and innovative, and how to be motivating and simultaneously be a member of the team as well. It was a tough road I had to take in my first leadership role, but I was lucky and had a great mentor as well as a great team, who helped me to learn, giving me feedback and allowing me to try things out. I realized very soon that there are countless leadership styles, approaches, models, and concepts, and I was simply overwhelmed by attempting to define which one was the best for me and my first leadership role.

There is a tricky aspect of leadership. Despite all these qualities and strengths that we are looking for in leaders, we also want them to be reflective and well aware of the situation, adjusting their actions accordingly. Thus the capacity to match and express core character strength in a way that is optimal in different situations is what is considered authentic leadership. It is less about being a type-A or type-B leader, because type A can be the best leadership style in a specific situation but could be absolutely wrong in another situation.

And why is this of relevance for you today? In the middle of the digital transformation, leadership is completely newly defined, with the number-one secret of excellent leaders being authentic leadership. Authentic leadership has much to do with being conscious, being aware of the situation, and being present. So authentic leadership is conscious leadership, and conscious leadership is really *the* most effective way of tackling complex challenges as we face them in a digital world—in a world at the edge of digital disruption. So the key message you need to remember here is that leadership is not about being perfect in one style or another, applying one model or another, or behaving in style A or style B. Really good digital leaders are authentic, and that means they are conscious of the situation, they are present in the moment, they realize what's going on, and they have the ability and the skill set to adapt to a specific situation.

There are plenty of textbook-style definitions of authentic leadership available, and they can be summarized by saying that we need the social/emotional skills to adapt to different people and situations, as well as the organizational context, in order to be more self-aware and have a positive influence on the people around us, leading to positive developments.

But what happens in a typical situation when leaders lack self-awareness? They tend to be less adaptable and swing toward one of the two opposite positions—compliance or defiance. To describe a leader in a defiant position is like drawing the picture of a person unconsciously focused on his/her own agenda, with a controlling and decisive style. This person is accompanied by a fear of failure and ignores others' needs. Maybe you have someone in mind who is always trying to push his or her agenda, who is a control freak and wants to decide and check everything, not giving permission until he or she has seen it. Many times these leaders are very much afraid of failing, and they neglect others' needs and focus only on what brings them forward, what's good for them.

Leaders who lack self-awareness and who are not authentic leaders at all can also swing in the other direction: compliance. A leader on the compliance side can be described as a person lacking spontaneity and having a fear of abandonment. This leader would typically be very eager to please others. And then in the middle we have the authentic leader who consciously balances the needs of self and others and acts adaptable and motivating.

Having had a look at the compliant and defiant leader, we can see that good digital leaders are active and positive in the way they behave in their world and how they interact with others. An authentic leader in the digital industry...

- *has a set of values in mind that represent an orientation toward doing what is right for their team, their department, and their organization. They truly believe that each individual has something positive to contribute.*
- *tries to work with no gap between their own true values and the values they use each day when working with others. So this means they are able not only to communicate their core values but also to behave according to those core values.*
- *is aware of his/her vulnerabilities and openly discusses them with associates. Why? Because they want to make sure they are going in the right direction. They*

are very transparent about what they can and cannot do, and they count on people's respect for knowing this and sharing it openly.

- *is a role model in confidence, hope, optimism, and resilience, which inspires others to such actions. It is about "walking the talk," and that is much more effective in keeping up the positive influence than trying to persuade somebody.*

- *very interested in building authenticity in their team members and helping them to find their personal best spot according to their capacity and strengths.*

Obviously, the ability of a leader to adapt to different situations is key, especially in the digital industry, with lots of changes happening fast. Being an authentic leader means you emphasize the importance of being highly reflective in order to judge the situation right and have the right reaction/style.

It is the sociable, open, and curious leaders who focus more on people and less on data and output. It is the leaders who are willing to put people first and technical and process-related issues second. It is the leaders who put their team first and have their personal radar scan other people's emotional states and react appropriately. These will be the leaders who master and succeed in the digital industry.

MASTERING RESILIENCE

Talking about "work" as part of the NOWING® methodology would not be complete if we left out "the big" topic that seems to be predominant in today's organizations across cultures and societies. Whether one is employed or unemployed, young or old, skilled or unskilled, stress is what all of us can relate to, with all kinds of different experiences. One could go over all the elements of stress—what causes stress, typical stressors, and so on—but it is more useful to talk about the number-one medicine for stress, which is called resilience.

By definition, *resilience* is the ability to withstand stress with minimum strain. We all know that there are external stress factors as well as internal ones. We also know that we can neither create a world without stress nor avoid stress at all. So the only way to improve our ability to deal with it is to allow for the least negative and best possible impact on us as organisms. The critical task, so to speak, is to strengthen our healthy ability to withstand unpleasant and potentially harmful situations with minimum impact on our physical and psychological functioning. In simple words: How well do we bounce back from any stress-related disturbance? How much of a tumbler are you?

Mother Nature built all different kinds of stress responses into our system; yes, that is absolutely right. Without our stress responses we wouldn't live for long, because our bodies would not adjust to heat/cold, pain, loneliness, or danger. So the physiological impact of stress on our system is absolutely helpful and affects our cardiovascular and musculoskeletal systems, our brain and skin, as well as our immune system. But stress is meant to be withstood for a short time span, and the trouble starts if stress becomes omnipresent, day in and day out, not allowing us as individuals to get off of the "hamster wheel."

In stressful situations people may experience a physiological change, such as increased blood pressure or reduced immune effectiveness. They may also experience a change in their emotions, feeling anxious, panicked, guilty, or worried all the time. Stressful situations can cause behavioral changes—from smoking to drinking, changed sleeping patterns, or simply aggressiveness.

So what we need are the skills of highly resilient people, who face the same stressors we face every day but who are capable of "bouncing back" from those disturbances much better. As diverse as we are as human beings, is as diverse as the range of potential activities, approaches, and strategies one can apply to improve one's personal level of resilience. It is a bit like building your new house. There are a trillion options on how to arrange the rooms, place the windows, and which furniture to use so you feel comfortable and can enjoy your privacy. If your unique resilience is like a house that provides you with shelter from the heavy storm and wind out in the real world, here are some ways to improve your resilient home:

- ***Add optimism*** *in how you see yourself and how you see the things around you: it is just a question of perspective, whether the glass is half-full or half-empty.*
- ***Add some focus on solutions*** *rather than on problems because creativity and openness always allow for new paths toward an answer.*

- **Add responsibility** and leave victimhood, without blaming others for what they are or aren't doing for you.
- **Add self-efficacy** and focus on your strengths, fully clear about your level of motivation and how you manage yourself.
- **Add acceptance** for things and circumstances you can't change, and take actions to change those you can in your favor.
- **Add network** by mastering empathy and engagement, and being in a vibrant social network.
- **Add future vision** so there is always a clear direction on where to go and why one option is better than the other.

Theoretical background on how to improve your current level of resilience is necessary to find a starting point but useless until you translate this knowledge to reality. It is less likely that stressors will disappear; rather, the frequency and forcefulness of their appearance will change. So there is one option to wait and see how your level of resilience remains at current levels or even decreases. Alternatively, you get ready to take the first step now and start improving your ability to "bounce back."

―――――――

* _Write down the top three adjustments you could make to protect or develop your resilience in the next three months in any of the outlined dimensions. As an example, you could work on your level of acceptance and not complain about the weather_ *every morning or about the traffic jam on the way to work. Both things you can't change but only accept (dimension: acceptance). Another area for improvement that's worth trying is the following: every time your team members or your boss present an idea or a task to you and you are tempted to say "that doesn't work because..." turn it around and try to look for a solution why/how it could work (dimension: focus on solution). Another very powerful exercise to fit easily into every day is to make it part of your morning routine to reaffirm yourself that you can accomplish what's ahead of you, that you trust in your abilities, and that you will manage whatever the day will present to you (dimension: self-efficacy).*

* *For each of the three identified adjustments, be specific—what do you want to try/achieve/do by when? Which resources are needed? What should be the effect?*

* *Share your list with one person—a friend, a coworker, your spouse—and jointly reflect on your top three adjustments and how you want to achieve them. Any additional remarks from your sparring partner?*

* *Adjust your initial plan after getting feedback from your sparring partner and create a short-term plan for making progress on those three.*

Although it should go without saying, it bears repeating: unless you implement your plan, your health and resilience won't improve. The sooner you start, the better you will be next time when a big storm of problems and challenges comes toward you.

DOING NOTHING

I still recall our ninety-plus-year-old neighbor, a lifelong farmer, saying, "There is always something to do" whenever you asked him about taking a break. Probably it was true in his case, with the duty to run a farm with plenty of animals 365 days a year. Nevertheless, he knew instinctively when it was time to rest, to stop a strenuous task and to take a break. On the contrary, many of us have lost this instinct but are conditioned to continue going like the little pink rabbit in the battery advertisement from some years ago. This behavior of not daring to rest sometimes goes back to teachings we have had during childhood, when we were taught "not to be lazy," to be "productive" and "to get something done."

Isn't it a real pleasure to do nothing every once in a while? Just listen to people talk about their vacation—most likely they tell you how great it was to master laziness. When we are asked to complete a task, for many people it is a natural habit to get going and to get it done within the given time frame. Being given the task to do nothing for half a day, or let's say for two hours only, causes some people to panic because they can't cope with doing nothing. Isn't it strange that this is too much of a challenge, although the "task" is not at all difficult?

As a matter of fact, it is essential that we build breaks into our days, weeks, and months as well as into our overall life. Breaks help our mind to regenerate, our senses to be sharp and receptive again, and they improve our overall ability to perform much better. If doing nothing is so difficult, here are at least some good starting points for improving your productive time:

Enjoy something nice instead of nothing. Especially during tough times we barely consider doing nothing and thus overlook the power of taking a short break and indulging ourselves in something nice. This could be a good dinner with your spouse, a visit to the movies with your best friend, or a glass of wine at your favorite Italian restaurant in town. Knowing that these kinds of little breaks—and "windows of retreat"—are essential, especially during busy times, schedule them in your calendar if you have difficulty making time for them on the fly.

Five minutes closed. What if you could go for a short vacation every day? All you need to do is allow yourself to close your eyes for five minutes, let your thoughts go on a journey to your favorite place, to the beach of your last vacation or to the marvelous view from the top of the mountain that you enjoyed so much during your last hiking trip.

A break as a habit. Whether it is the famous coffee break that you celebrate once or twice a day and for which you stop work for few minutes, or you have a cup of tea—whatever ritual you can incorporate best into your daily routine, make sure it is one that allows your mind and your body to relax for a moment from all work-related activities. What many high-performing individuals from different disciplines practice as a routine is their ninety-day-retreat. Mark your calendar and take at least two or three days off every ninety days and allow your mind and body to take a break, to recharge, and to relax. This is one of my personal favorites, and it works like a miracle for me to know that in less than ninety days the next retreat is coming up.

Don't fall into the trap of recreational stress. Just because at work you are going crazy with too many things to do and with too little time available, it doesn't mean you should also try to work out, swim, and run a marathon every other day during these busy times. If you face peak season at work—which is not to be a permanent condition.—you should not plan for peak performance in your spare time as well.

Making room for these simple ideas for doing more of nothing isn't difficult and should become a priority for you. If you are asking yourself where you can make time for that, it is sometimes the little practice of saying "no" that makes the difference. With every "no" to a task presented, you create some more room for potentially doing nothing.

Saying "no" seems to be a horrible thing for many people, as they fear hurting others, not being loved anymore, or being excluded. First and foremost, keep in mind that you can only give if you feel good, and not if you feel like a Ping-Pong ball for other people's agendas. Second, keep in mind that every discussion has a content level and a relationship level. Saying "no" on the first doesn't mean "no" on the latter. Try to estimate realistically what a "no" really implies and what could happen if you turn somebody's request down. For those of you struggling frequently with the word "no," it might help if you explain the reasons for saying no or if you have some sentences ready to use, such as:

- *If I do something, I want to do it right. I don't have the time right now so it would not be wise for me to take on X.*
- *I am happy to help next time / next week but not this time.*
- *It has nothing to do with you / with the topic X, but those things I can't do at all.*
- *If I do this, I will be under real time pressure.*
- *I haven't had much time with my family / my friends / with X lately, thus I would focus my priorities there right now.*

If all the necessary skills such as solving problems, leading authentically, and being mindful are necessary for working in the digital industry, the question remains: What else is needed? Is there something else needed at all? Can the mere application and mastery of skills improve individual performance, or are there additional parameters that are also essential for achieving a state of excellent performance?

I would argue that it is less a question of which additional skills are potentially of importance or how well someone is capable of handling one of these critical skills. For me it is more a question of how we approach learning and the acquisition of new skills. Start-ups are great examples of how organizations as well as individuals should design their approach to learning new skills and to working in the digital industry. First there is a problem that needs to be solved. Then the start-up team builds a business model around this problem that is capable of addressing the issue more effectively and creating value on top. During this journey each individual and the entire team is challenged to work better, learn more, and realize their full potential. They find new, innovative ways of working and collaborating and adjust their skill sets, tools, and capabilities along the journey to best serve their mission. Once we fully understand that work equals learning and learning is work, we are on the right track.

CHECKPOINT ON WORK

Below you will find the key questions and thoughts related to this chapter, and your free workbook is waiting to be downloaded at www.braininspa.com.

---

* *For future problem solving, I will start asking the four questions about situation, complications, key questions, and the possible breakdown of the issue presented.*

_____

_____

_____

_____

_____

_____

* *For complex issues, I use the following technique/model to take it apart...*

_____

_____

_____

_____

_____

_____

* *Being more of an authentic leader, I will consider the following adjustments in my leadership role over the next three months...*

_____

_____

_____

_____

_____

_____

* *Building my "house of resilience" means for me...*

_____

_____

_____

_____

_____

* *My "window of retreats" this week is...and it's planned for...*

_____

_____

_____

_____

_____

_____

* *Saying "no" is not difficult anymore for me because...*

_____
_____
_____
_____
_____
_____

* *To bring more start-up mentality to my work / my job I will do...*

_____
_____
_____
_____
_____
_____

_____

Nine

Element 4:
INTERACT

As humans we are meant to collaborate, to join forces, to interact with one another. We are not made to live as lone warriors. From the early days we were not meant to survive as individuals but as part of a group, a family, a network of like-minded people with shared values. We were meant to care for others, deeply, and by doing so we tend to get what we want because others see us as compassionate and kind, so they reciprocate.

The basis for our caring and the ability to interact is our people skills. When we give others time, attention, and caring, they admire us, respect us, and help us in return. It's the kindness and generosity that draws people in and helps us achieve high performance. We should see it as our duty to master this ability to give and take, to be with other people in influential ways, to be good role models. Once we manage this, others naturally want to be part of our team, support us, and ultimately help us achieve even higher levels of performance.

All great people skills start with the ability to communicate, verbally as well as nonverbally. To have others follow us and support our mission, we need to master our ability to persuade and to influence. We need to adjust our style of interacting with our network of colleagues, friends, and family in a way that demonstrates strong emotional intelligence if we want to make a difference.

COMMUNICATIONS BASICS

Isn't it communication that we are practicing day in and day out, from being a few months old till hopefully far beyond our ninetieth birthday? Yes, it is communication, but there is a big difference between being effective communicators and great chatterboxes. It is the ability to clearly articulate an idea, a question, a proposal, or a solution that makes the difference. To identify easily the main message, key points, and supporting messages is part of a great communicator's toolkit, as well the capability to outline a logical storyboard with the corresponding facts and figures. Communication has been essential to humans not only because it is one of the key differentiators between *Homo sapiens* and other species. Communication is also one of the most critical skills required to survive and to achieve high performance in the digital industry: whether this verbal/nonverbal/written exchange takes place in a real, human-to-human interaction or in a virtual way does not matter as long as the message goes through as intended.

There is no such thing as a perfect communicator. Some people are great at speaking and interacting with a specific type of person or group; others may be excellent on a special subject. What they all learned to master, however, is structuring their thoughts in a way that is easy to understand and for their audience to follow. Whatever message you have to share, make sure you are obeying these seven golden rules:

- *I am clear about what I say.*
- *I am concise and stick to the point.*
- *I provide my audience with a concrete, vivid picture of what I am saying.*
- *I provide error-free, correct messages.*
- *I provide complete information—all the content my audience needs to know.*
- *I use a friendly, open, and honest style.*
- *I use a coherent, logical structure.*

All communication efforts start with the key message we want to deliver. It is like the one-sentence summary of our thoughts, ideas, recommendations, or concerns. This main message at the top of any communication is accompanied by three to five key supportive points, primary reasons why we believe the main message is true. So these are supportive arguments, facts, and figures. At the bottom of the message we have an even broader base of "supportive data"—information that proves why the above-mentioned arguments are true.

And why is it that we should start our communication efforts with the key message from the top and not by explaining all the supportive data we have collected first? Because people, especially high performers, are trained to be precise, to hear the key message first and to understand what the topic is all about and then get the underlying facts and figures presented subsequently.

Yes, there are a gazillion options on how to optimize and improve your communication. Yes, there are nuances, whether you communicate verbally one-on-one, in front of a larger audience, in writing, or in a chat forum. Regardless of your channel, your topic, or your audience, the better you structure, the clearer you are, the more of a great communicator you will become. And communication in any medium is one of the most strategic skills needed for high performance in the digital space.

PERSUADE THEM—YOUR WAY

To communicate and to interact with others is only the starting point, however. If we want to develop ourselves toward better performance we need to focus on how to influence and persuade others so they are more willing to support our arguments, our ideas, and our plans, thus helping us achieve our objectives.

Persuasion is critical in almost any endeavor, from negotiations in a professional setting to simply asking your kids to clean up their rooms. The answer to the question of how we can motivate others to believe or behave in a certain way rests upon four pillars:

Clarity: You need to be clear what you want to achieve, what the ultimate goal is that you require others to support you with. You need to understand their "dialect"—what is the world of pictures, words, and situations they are familiar with; what are the stories that resonate well with them; and what are the arguments they can relate to because of their background, current situation, or level of interest on the subject?

Honor: You need to honor, acknowledge, and appreciate others for the struggles and challenges they have already been through and that they managed to overcome, to survive, and ideally to master. You must honor their success from the past before you can present a new request to them.

Vision: When you want others to support and follow your mission, answer their question "What's in it for me?" Provide them with the necessary information that feeds their ambition for a better future. This could be anything from personal mission and enjoyment to monetary rewards, popularity, or fame. Tell them what they will get by following your path and how their actions will bring them greater results.

Emotion: Communication only works in terms of providing honor for what one has achieved and providing vision for what one can get if it is done with the right level of emotion. And I mean a high dose of emotion. That's what is needed. Use your tone and your stories; if you want others to move your way, be empathetic and touch base with them on an emotional level and you have paid more than half the rent.

Done right, the four pillars of persuasion will tremendously support you in getting more and more followers and supporters—online and in the real world. What many over-look, however, is one of the biggest secrets of successful in-fluencing: telling and teaching others how and what to think. This might sound like a bit too much of a directive style here, but think about it for a moment. The more articulate and ex-plicit you are in sharing with others how and what you want them to think, feel, and focus on, the more you can shape their point of view and their life. Imagine you are a team leader and tell your team that there is a project coming up that they will manage easily, and within a few weeks they can celebrate a great success story. If you then honor their current skill sets, remind them of how well they have handled similar requests in the past, help them paint a vision of what great things can happen if this one specific project for this new client works out and where the follow-up sales could lead you as a team, and you deliver all of this with emotion, showing real apprecia-tion for your team members' work and truly believing in them, well, there isn't much that could go wrong.

WORKING WITH HUMANS

Having analyzed what is ahead of us in terms of disruptive technologies and digital challenges, the importance of peo-ple skills can't be stressed enough—individuals who interact well on teams, who master flexibility, and who are able to ad-just to change quickly. They will be the key talents in the fu-ture years in any industry.

There is no correlation between number of degrees or qualifications one possesses and the emotional qualities needed to succeed. The more you understand your own strengths and weaknesses and how certain behavior affects others, the higher your level of self-awareness. The more intrinsically motivated and self-motivated someone shows up, the more resilience is in place and the better the overall team performance will be. The more mature a person is in expressing emotions, the higher the level of self-regulation. The more one has the ability to relate to others, to connect and empathize, the easier it is for them to build trust, rapport, and respect in the long run. Is this a shift that is more in favor of younger generations? Yes, for sure, simply because it reflects more on how they have been raised compared to the upbringing of baby boomers or generation X. Emotional intelligence is not like degrees and qualifications: you don't need a long period of study or years of education and a formal degree confirming you have accomplished your goals. Being a good, a better, or a perfect people person is something you can—and should—practice each and every day. There are plenty of opportunities out there waiting for more people-focused individuals.

So the good news is that you can also learn to improve your people skills. But how? A good starting point is to analyze yourself: How do you react to people? Are you the first one stereotyping or are you open and ready to place yourself in their shoes, trying to understand and potentially accept their perspective? People with good emotional intelligence also practice putting others first and themselves second—at least sometimes. We all like to shine and seek attention for our accomplishments, but there are also others we should give a fair share of appreciation. Giving others room to shine can also mean that we need to accept that we can't be perfect and that there are still areas we need to work on. Yes, it takes courage to look in the mirror and be honest with yourself about finding out where your areas for improvement are.

One area you can always strengthen is your reaction in stressful situations: Are you going crazy because of a delay or unplanned problems with a project? Is it the others' fault that things went wrong? Or do you stay calm and focused on the topic and avoid pointing fingers or searching for who's to blame?

Improving people skills is also about practicing taking responsibility for your actions and learning to say "I'm sorry" if you did something wrong. Raise your level of interest in others, practice placing yourself in their situation, and make sure there is a human touch to your daily interactions, and your people skills will improve tremendously.

CHECKPOINT ON INTERACT
Here are your key questions and thoughts for this chapter, and the free workbook can be downloaded at www.braininspa.com:

———

* *My next communication (e-mail, one-on-one) I will structure along the seven golden rules of great communicators, which are...*

  _____

  _____

  _____

  _____

  _____

  _____

* *In order to persuade more people in my life, I will focus on clarity by doing...honor by doing...vision by doing...and emotion by doing...*

  _____

  _____

  _____

  _____

  _____

  _____

* *The way I normally react to people is...*

_____

_____

_____

_____

_____

_____

* *I will practice putting myself in someone else's shoes next time by doing...*

_____

_____

_____

_____

_____

_____

* *If there is an unplanned event that causes me stress, next time I will try to make things better by doing...*

_____

_____

_____

_____

_____

_____

*   I will make myself more responsible for what I am doing, will be willing to say "sorry" the next time...happens.

_____

_____

_____

_____

_____

_____

_____

Ten

Element 5:
NURTURE

If we take the time to organize our environment, manage our productivity, and master our interactions with others, it would be crazy if we did not start with us, our own body, first. We need to care for ourselves first, our mind and our body if we want to act in the best interest of our health and our overall life. Without caring for us, we can't ensure a high level of well-being, thus we take away the basis for sustained high performance.

Sometimes we are so busy handling daily requests, serving loved ones, and pleasing friends and colleagues, that there is not much room and time for us. So we put ourselves last. That's the reason most people don't have a healthy body and a healthy mind but struggle with all kinds of lifestyle-related diseases such as obesity, insomnia, or different levels of burnout.

Feeling energetic, having the power to perform with a high level of engagement and productivity doesn't happen overnight. It needs at least a little effort and, above all, commitment from you personally that you want to make change happen, that you are serious about implementing small changes to help your body and your mind reach a heightened level of performance, thus helping you to make a giant leap to a life full of charge, joy, and happiness.

To nurture in the context of NOWING® not only covers how we feed our body but also how we feed our mind. Thus NURTURE runs along four key dimensions—motion, food, presence, and cognition. Let's make it a priority to become a guard for ourselves, a guard for how we feed our body, and a guard for all the information, thoughts, and emotions we allow into our mind. It's not that we need new diets or new scientific findings that we had to wait for before getting started with a healthier life. It's all here, and it is probably not new information for many of you, either. But what is definitely new for many people who want to move toward real high performance is the true commitment and focus on the most essential elements when caring for your body and mind.

UNDERSTANDING THE MIND-BODY TALK

Without a doubt it is our mind that allows us—once understood, nourished, and used in the right way—to handle all the changes and challenges we face daily. In medical school, doctors learn that there are two kinds of people: sick people and well people. The sick people obviously have something wrong with them physically; there might be some abnormal radiology or laboratory test results. To help solve their problem, doctors prescribe them some medication and hope to keep them from getting any worse disease or—worst-case scenario—dying. Maybe they are good doctors who manage their patients to the point at which they, for example, change their health-affecting behavior, ask them to exercise more, lose weight, or do whatever is needed to improve their medical circumstances. And then there is the category of patients who are in between: they are neither sick nor well. Technically speaking, everything is OK with them: their lab test results are all OK; their blood pressure doesn't cause any worries. But still, they don't feel well—and nobody can help them. What's wrong with them? What are they suffering from? They are suffering from the physiological consequences of their body's stress response. Yes, your thoughts can have physical impact on your body, or, in other words, your mind talks to your body.

Let's just imagine for a second that you are afraid of something. Let's assume a doctor tells you that you have only five months to live. Or maybe it is something less life-threatening but still fearful. Let's say you are afraid of getting fired at the end of this month. So your conscious mind, located in your forebrain, knows about your current feeling and the anticipated catastrophe. But your lizard brain—the area that houses the hypothalamus—can't tell the difference between a "real" fear and an imagined/potential threat. So it creates a stress response that triggers the famous fight-or-flight reaction in your body, starting your sympathetic nervous system, reducing your immune system, getting everything ready to run away from the fictitious mountain lion—the one our ancestors faced when they felt real fear.

Our stressors today are much less life-threatening than a mountain lion, but our brain can't distinguish between being under real attack and "just" facing loneliness, unhappy relationships, financial worries, or stress at work. The response in our body is the same: increased pulse rate; constricting blood vessels in your belly, hands, and feet; increased respiratory rate; and so on. In short, your body does not opt for sleeping, digesting, or reproducing but instead prepares for running, producing, running, producing, and running. If your body remains in this state for too long or gets into this state too often, it can't relax and repair itself anymore. Your body will become more and more ill, or at least able to perform less and less well.

Does it have to be this way? No. Not at all. When we feed our conscious forebrain with positive thoughts such as love, relatedness, pleasure, hope, and connectedness, the stress response is stopped, cortisol and adrenaline levels drop, and the body can go back to its normal self-repair process. So no pills or drugs are needed.

There is a counterbalance to the fight-or-flight response: the body's state of quietude, which allows it to repair the damage caused by stress. Intuitively many of us know when we are stressed out and when our body screams for relaxation.

Unfortunately, many of us don't take the best medication for life stress—namely meditation or mindfulness exercises. Rather, we go for a drink, enjoy a smoke, or take some medication in order to get a pseudorelaxation response. Going down this wrong path causes your body even more stress, doing even more harm, especially on a physiological level. Whether your body whispers or screams for relaxation, make sure you choose the right path down the mindfulness track.

HAVE YOUR MIND FULLY IN THE PRESENT

Whether you are looking for simple relaxation, heightened awareness or better concentration, the way forward remains the same—you need to train your brain for a state of consciousness, being in the present, being here and now. Imagine your heart beats at one hundred forty beats per minute for a long period of time—wouldn't you be worried, exhausted, sweating, and fatigued? It is the same for your brain: you need to allow for a timeout with less stress, for reducing the speed of your brain toward a healthier brain wave activity level in the alpha range of eight to twelve hertz instead of racing in the beta range above twenty-five hertz.

There is a broad variety of techniques and exercises available that can help you achieve this state of relaxation and attentional focus. You could practice simple breathing exercises or repeat your personal mantra. The little word "OM" is the most famous one that brings monks to a relaxed state of mind. You could also practice some simple mindfulness techniques or engage in different levels of meditation exercises. The benefits you will enjoy are probably bigger and more far-reaching than you imagine—you will feel your stress level drop, as all mindfulness activities also affect your cortisol levels. Different regions in your brain will operate more in harmony, like a well-rehearsed band, allowing you to perform cognitive tasks better, faster, and with less distraction. Your sleep will improve, and the same is true for your immune system. And if you are currently worried about your cardiovascular health, meditation will have a positive effect on your blood pressure and also help you slow your heartbeat.

When it comes to regulating your emotions and focusing your attention, any mindfulness exercise will help, depending on how frequently you practice. There are many great resources and meditation guides available. I have posted one of my personal favorites as a *free* download for you at www. braininspa.com.

Speaking of practice, the key question remaining is "How?" How often should you practice what should you practice in order to reap the benefits? It all depends on your starting point, whether you are completely new to mindfulness exercises or are currently practicing meditation several times a week or have already completed a yoga or tai chi course. If you are starting out, make sure you have a simple breathing exercise as part of your daily routine, and after two or three weeks you should try one or two short (twenty- to thirty-minute) meditation exercises a week. Once you are more experienced and feel the positive impact on your body, your awareness, and your level of relaxation, increase the number of meditation exercises to three to five per week or consider upgrading to a regular yoga or tai chi program. Following this path and incorporating these new techniques and exercises as a habit in your daily life will allow your body to relax and recharge much better—and as a result allow you to be more energetic, focused, and present in the moment.

A PLATE FOR BODY AND MIND

There is no need to spend paragraphs and pages on nutrition, good diet, and healthy eating habits…or maybe there is. Most of us know what we should put on our plate, what we should leave off, what we should eat less of, when we should eat what, and which ingredients are better than others. Isn't it mind-blowing to keep an overview and not to get trapped in the healthy-eating jungle? It asks too much of the general public to manage all the advice offered and to create structure and clarity in our daily food planning. As a result, many people quit, eat what they have a craving for, and prefer the convenience of processed food…and then they wonder why their levels of well-being, performance, and energy go down.

Nurturing your body and your mind in a healthy way is neither mind-blowing nor should it be complicated. Of course there is always room to fine-tune, and I can only encourage you to get a personal nutritionist, test all your essential vitamin levels and your important blood parameters, and create an absolutely individualized food plan that is optimized for you, your body, and your lifestyle.

Yes, it takes a while to get to this level, and yes, one needs to be able to afford this in terms of money and time. The good news is, however, that there is a more practical, affordable way forward, a way you can start today, right now, with very small effort and time investment. You can take a big step forward toward a healthy body and higher performance if you just take care of the *five nurture basics*. Implementing these five in your daily routine right away will give you a good boost in the right direction. And if you then want more, you can always go to the next level.

———

(1) **Sleep.** *Make sure you get seven or eight hours of sleep each night, because a rested body is the baseline for performance. Without enough sleep you can nurture yourself with all good ingredients, but your internal system simply won't be rested enough to make use of all the good stuff you put in. Sleeping time is also renewal time for your body, needed for muscle repair, memory consolidation, and release of hormones regulating growth and appetite.*

(2) **Drink water.** *Make sure you are hydrated well by drinking around two liters (about eight cups or sixty-six ounces) of water a day. Because this can be a difficult task, make sure you create a habit around drinking water. I personally make sure I have half a liter of fresh juice and coffee or tea for breakfast. Then I don't allow myself to go for lunch if I haven't finished the one-liter carafe of water at my desk,*

and I fill up the same carafe with a second liter for the afternoon right after lunch.

(3) **Eat organic.** *Focus on organic food. Whenever you can—and yes, despite the higher price—it is absolutely critical to consume organic food, ideally from your own garden, a community garden project, or a local organic farmer. Try to avoid those perfectly shaped, almost red-yellow-colored apples that were treated with multiple doses of pesticides to get a perfect look. Rather, enjoy the real taste of apples and pears right off the tree without any chemicals. Keep in mind, the toxic substances they use to make the fruits and vegetables look perfect are then part of your diet— and this is not good for you. By the way, organic shouldn't be for veggies and fruits alone but, even more importantly, the meat and dairy products you consume.*

(4) **Cook it yourself.** *Start out with once a week that you prepare a meal for yourself and your family or for friends at home, all by yourself, not using any processed food, nothing pre-cooked or "ready-to-eat" out of the freezer. Enjoy cutting the vegetables; spend the time talking to your kids, your spouse; enjoy the delicious smell of fresh-cooked food that is all over your house. Push yourself to two or three or maybe five or six home-cooked main meals a week, and make it a rare thing to eat out. Home-cooking takes time, so also allow for enough time to eat, and then ensure your table is nicely set; chat and socialize with family or friends while enjoying your home-cooked meal.*

(5) **Cover the essential seven.** *Regardless of your preferred meals, vegetables, and fruits, there is a list of my personal*

"secret seven" that I recommend you regularly include in your diet if you want to improve your performance, especially your cognitive abilities:

* *omega-3 fatty acids that come from fish oil or algal sources*
* *apples (you know the saying: "an apple a day keeps the*
  doctor away")
* *blueberries: pure, not covered with sugar in blueberry muffins*
* *tomatoes: like in a delicious Greek salad, not canned as sauce for your pizza margherita*
* *red grapes: natural but also as a glass of wine once in a while*
* *nuts: known as the best brain snack in case of snack attack*
* *black and green tea: a perfect substitute for your second cup of coffee in the afternoon*

Once you implement these five nurture basics, your diet will improve significantly and so will your performance. Of course there are a multitude of tips and hints for a healthy diet and special plans available. But it is always easier to start with small steps first, steps that you probably do not consider a 180-degree shift from the status quo. Once you have mastered these basics, feel free to continue fine-tuning how you feed your body and your brain in the optimal way to ensure even better functioning. Whether you take online courses on healthy diets, a vegetarian cooking course, or buy some new books with delicious, healthy, and easy-to-cook family meals, push yourself and keep in mind that what you eat is the basis for your body's performance—physically and mentally.

PRACTICE FOR MOTION AND COGNITION

Any form of exercise—whether it is going for a walk or running a marathon—affects the body. The same is true for the mind. Recent studies show that our brain is like a muscle—the more we train and challenge our neurons and synapses, the better, faster, and brighter they perform. But let's start with physical exercise first, before we look into how to train our neurons and synapses.

With any form of exercise it is true that one is better than zero. So it doesn't have to be a marathon you are preparing for; it is also a step in the right direction if you go for an extended walk every other day and build this over a two- or three-week period into a thirty-minute jogging session three times a week, and eventually you will be able to complete a short-distance-running exercise two to four times a week. Wow! It all starts with commitment to change your current exercise level and taking little steps instead of one giant step, which can frustrate you if you can't do it.

At this point it is not the intention of the NOWING® model to serve as a fitness guide—there are plenty of special resources out there—but to raise awareness of how important exercising your body and your mind is in order to improve your well-being and performance. Any form of physical exercise improves your cardiovascular health, increasing "good cholesterol" levels in the blood. It also boosts the creation of new blood vessels in the brain, thus securing a better oxygen supply.

It isn't only physical exercise that contributes to a large extent to your overall performance. It is also any form of cognitive stimulation and practicing specific activities that allow the connections in our brain to improve, even to enlarge certain brain regions. The logic here is simple: your overall performance will improve with practice, because as you challenge your brain with specific exercises, you add and strengthen your neurons and synapses.

The question asked most is, "Which exercises help my 'brain muscle' to grow and in return help to push my performance?" In general one can say that the harder you make your brain work, the better it gets and the bigger the benefit. The little exercises and the small steps add up and help build or at least maintain the "muscle."

Easy activities to increase the performance of your brain are, for example, playing puzzles (maybe with your children), an easy Sudoku, or learning new subjects (take, for example, an online course). The next level in terms of difficulty—or "brain workout"—would be specific brain-teasing games, geocaching or learning to dance. If you are ready for the expert level, you should be able to memorize, for example, a deck of cards (yes, there are even competitions for that), learn a new language in a few months' time, or even go back to college and get another or your first degree. All this will mean a terrific workout for your brain and will not only provide you with the ability to perform above your peer group but also give you pleasure and help you avoid a truckload of common "brain-related" diseases that people face who retire mentally long before their sixty-fifth birthday.

It is not the complexity or the difficulty that keeps many people away from nurturing their body and their mind in the right way. It's simply a lack of understanding the basics combined with never taking the first step of making change happen. Now that you have read about the importance and the different ways of being a good guard to yourself, you can call yourself educated enough to understand those basics. The only step that keeps you away from enjoying more productivity, energy, clarity, and performance is simply getting started.

CHECKPOINT ON NURTURE

The key questions and thoughts related to this chapter are outlined below, and your free workbook is available for download at www.braininspa.com:

———————

* *To counteract my body's stress response, I can enjoy more love, relatedness, pleasure, and hope by doing/starting/ intensifying...*

———————————————————
———————————————————
———————————————————
———————————————————
———————————————————
———————————————————

* *To practice mindfulness I will start with a simple breathing exercise for this week by doing...*

———————————————————
———————————————————
———————————————————
———————————————————
———————————————————
———————————————————

* *To sleep seven or eight hours each night. I need to go to bed at...in order to get up at my scheduled time of...*

  _____

  _____

  _____

  _____

  _____

  _____

* *Drinking two liters of water each day. I will complete by doing...*

  _____

  _____

  _____

  _____

  _____

  _____

* *I can substitute the following foods with organic ones:...*

  _____

  _____

  _____

  _____

  _____

  _____

* As of this week, I commit to making x meals a week at home by myself.

  _____

  _____

  _____

  _____

  _____

  _____

* To cover the "essential seven," I will make sure to include...in this week's diet.

  _____

  _____

  _____

  _____

  _____

  _____

* In case I am closer to being a "couch potato" than to being a "marathon junkie," I will start this week with more physical exercise by doing...

  _____

  _____

  _____

  _____

  _____

  _____

* *I will start building my "brain muscle" by doing...*

_____

_____

_____

_____

_____

_____

_____

Eleven

Element 6: GOAL

This chapter is last simply because it is about the final letter of the word "NOWING®": G, as in GOAL. Nevertheless, it should come first when you start working on improving your performance and your health. If the direction, the ultimate dream state of your life, and the purpose is clear, it is much easier to define the right steps to help you reach this goal. Before defining your personal picture of the future, however, most people need to take another, even more important step: raising the awareness that change is needed and generating real commitment to making change happen.

IT ALL STARTS WITH CHANGE

If you want something more out of life, if you want to acquire something, if there is some goal you seriously want to reach, it is very likely that you will need to change. That's a challenge, but it can be done. Thousands of people who were willing to achieve their goal and who were committed to making change happen have done it already. So can you.

It all starts in your mind because there is nothing as effective as a changed mind, a mind changed from distraction and confusion to focus and clarity. You can change your clothing, your partner, your address, and your house. But if you don't change your mind, you will have the same experiences over and over again, because even though everything changed externally, nothing inside you changed.

So why is it that people think change takes a long time? Maybe they have tried it with mere willpower and failed? Maybe their set of beliefs prevented them from allowing change to happen fast? Obviously if one can change in an instant, the problem never really existed or wasn't big enough, right? Launching a new endeavor and making real progress toward any goal, mastering high performance, always starts with understanding how you can make change happen and last.

First, if you want things to be different in the future, you must take responsibility: it is not others who are responsible for your change taking place; it is *you* who needs to be committed and to really want to achieve what you have on your dream agenda. Second, if you are serious about going for long-term change, you need to make sure that you reinforce that change once it's started. It is a bit like wanting to lose weight and going to the fitness club. If you show up there only once saying something like, "Hey, now I have a great body, am in shape, and weigh fifteen pounds less" that won't make you a size smaller. But if you keep going, keep practicing, and adjust your habits and rituals, gradually change will happen. For change to happen, it is essential to understand and execute the following:

---

* *Ask yourself what it is that you really want and what is preventing you now from having it.*
* *Change your patterns and behaviors by associating real pain and discomfort with the present situation (if no change is happening), and extreme pleasure and great feelings if change happens.*
* *Celebrate as if you were beyond that pain threshold of the above already. Paint a lively picture in your mind of your future state after change has happened.*
* *If you fall back into old habits—the ones that hinder you from achieving your goal—make sure you replace them with better alternatives.*
* *Keep practicing: whatever new habits, rituals, practices, and exercises you have started in order to make change happen and take giant leaps toward your goal, you need to keep repeating, repeating, and repeating them. On average it takes 30 days to install a new habit successfully!*
* *Celebrate—again—every time you are able to replace old habits with new behavior. Congratulate yourself for making*

it all the way through, and take this achievement as the best guarantee that you are capable of completing the rest of the journey.

THE *WHY* BEHIND YOUR LIFE

Managing change and truly creating commitment for your new endeavor is one thing, but it's almost impossible if you haven't constructed a proper answer for the *why* behind your life: What's your life's purpose?

Unfortunately, the majority of people living today live lives of mediocrity: they have a mediocre professional life, live in average homes in more or less average neighborhoods, spend an average of 1.5 hours a day with family members and children, and face some or all of life's challenges that 80 percent of this mediocre crowd experiences. To escape every once in a while from this average life they go on trips, take a few days off for vacation, or get some additional stimulation from even worse things like watching television, drinking alcohol, or eating excessive amounts of food. And when their time is over, they suddenly start asking themselves what it was that they lived for. What was their purpose, and did they live up to this bigger calling in their life? Can you imagine looking back from this final day—whenever it may be for you—and saying with pride:

Yes, this was my life. I am proud and happy with what I have accomplished, with the person I was, the unique skills I could bring to the table, how I made an impact for the better, and the way I connected and interacted with others. I knew there was a bigger reason, a real purpose for me being here. I did hear this call, and I answered it with pride and my highest self.

When you are reading those lines, it might be a sign to start thinking, because it is never too late to make a change and work more toward your life's purpose. It is not only millennials searching for the bigger meaning in what they are doing, it is necessary for all generations these days to search for the purpose in one's life. So start to answer these questions:

----

* *Who are you truly?*
* *Why are you here?*
* *What is your mission all about?*

Again, my favorite, Viktor Frankl, once said, "Ever more people today have the means to live, but no meaning to live for." Without meaning you can't make proper decisions about whether going left or right is better. You can't even define good objectives and a path that you would like to take if you have no clue where these objectives would lead you. But with meaning, with a clear understanding for the purpose of your life, you are ready to live a charged, powerful, and happy life, enjoying the present and the beauty life has in store for you and, most importantly, reaching your highest levels of performance and health.

YOUR PERSONAL MISSION

You know that most people go through life and never discover what their talents are, where their strengths are, what they do really well, and what they actually want in life. And they don't even develop their talents. It's even worse than that: they don't even have a goal they want to achieve.

And then you see people who are extremely successful and you think, Wow, I am jealous; how did they do that? Those are the ones who are rewarded in public for what they practiced over and over again for years.

Now it is your turn to develop the courage to do what you are meant to be doing and to stop pleasing and serving others, helping them only with their agenda. It all comes down to the winner's quality: winners hold on despite everything, they are creative and committed to their goals, and they learn the power to endure. They possess this special power that is so difficult to describe. Winners are privileged in the way in which they know exactly who they are and what they want; they are fully determined not to quit until they finish and succeed. How can you do the same? You must focus on yourself and what your goals are. Yes, this is your life, and yes, you can achieve your dream, your goal, if you are focused and take action. Now.

The good news is that setting goals is not at all difficult, and you have no doubt heard about the concept of setting

SMART goals. SMART is an acronym that stands for *specific, measurable, achievable, realistic, and time-bound*. If you quality-test your goals against these five attributes, you will be better off than many others. But there is more you can do to make your dream come true.

For defining a goal according to the NOWING® Formula, the five SMART criteria are not enough. Apply the following checklist, and your goals will serve your life's purpose even better:

———————

* *Make your goal challenging enough. Being overwhelmed and almost paralyzed doesn't help much. A great goal gets you excited, engaged, and connected.*
* *Make your goal significant so it gets your full concentration and is worth absolute attention, not leaving you bored or easily distracted.*
* *Make sure your goal is above the comfort-zone line so it requires you to stretch and expand your skills and capabilities.*
* *Make sure you can track progress of how much you have already achieved toward your goal.*
* *Make sure there is a finish line for each goal; otherwise you won't endure the stretch of a challenging goal.*
* *Make sure you have high-quality, nontoxic company on the way toward your goal—someone to help you to evaluate, to motivate, and, finally, to celebrate when you reach your goal.*

———————

Once your ambitious objectives are SMART and adhere to the above checklist, you can be certain that achieving them is worth all the effort. But it is not only the final destination, the ultimate goal, the outcome that you should focus on. It is also the journey, the hiking trail that takes you closer and closer to your goal. There might be fears and doubts along the way; you might come across some unmet expectations and the fear of being rejected. That's all part of the journey.

But if you are crystal clear about why you want what you want (your life's purpose) and what you want to achieve (your goals), all these roadblocks won't do any harm to your journey.

And what about the critics? The ones who are extremely skilled and partially successful and making us feel unsure, distracted, worried? Don't give them power over you, your life, and your goal. Simply ignore them and consider them the weak ones, the ones who don't have their own goal they can strive for so they keep themselves busy criticizing other ambitious individuals like you. Simply ignore them.

Once we start thinking about our purpose and our goals in life, we might feel a bit overwhelmed by the number of goals identified. Supposedly there are some goals related to your health, some related to your job or professional life, some related to your private life, and some about the environment you live and work in. Dealing with all of them at once is not a good idea and maybe not even possible. Rather, break them down and sequence them: you could do a yearly planning process to define which goals from different aspects of your life—family, sports, business, hobby, etc.—you want to focus on first. Then dedicate one month to a specific objective: January could be your month for focusing on eating habits; February, your month to polish your negotiation skills; March is about prioritizing and structuring your day...and it might all add up to your bigger goal about launching your own start-up within the next year.

If you think about a Christmas tree for a moment, you have a picture of something green in your mind, something with lots of different colorful decorations on it, right? In your mind, place your biggest, your ultimate goal, your strategic objective on the top of this Christmas tree and place all the subgoals on the branches underneath. The decoration is all about your achievements and reminds you to celebrate every time you have completed a subgoal. Then start a journey from the bottom of the roots to the top of the tree, going after one goal at a time, climbing to the next level of branches and the next level of goals. Make sure your skills and the intensity of the challenge are well balanced and you can be certain that you will reach the top of the tree and enjoy a marvelous view.

CHECKPOINT ON GOAL

Are you ready for the key questions and thoughts related to this chapter? If you need a bit of structure to help you think, then download your free workbook at www.braininspa.com.

---

*   *I understand that change needs to happen first, before starting to define my vision and goals. So what I really want to happen/ achieve is...*

_____

_____

_____

_____

_____

_____

*   *What is preventing me from having this now is...*

_____

_____

_____

_____

_____

_____

* *I will change my patterns and associate real pain with the present situation, which means in detail...*

  _____

  _____

  _____

  _____

  _____

  _____

* *I will change my patterns and associate real pleasure with the changed situation by doing...*

  _____

  _____

  _____

  _____

  _____

  _____

* *If I come across old habits such as...I will replace them with better alternatives such as...*

  _____

  _____

  _____

  _____

  _____

  _____

*   *Whenever I manage to change a habit or a practice sustainably, I celebrate and congratulate myself by doing...*

_____

_____

_____

_____

_____

_____

*   *My life's purpose is...*

_____

_____

_____

_____

_____

*   *In the search for my life's purpose, I answer the question "Who am I?" with...the question "Why am I here?" with...and complete the statement "My mission is all about..."*

_____

_____

_____

_____

_____

_____

* *All my bigger and smaller goals will undergo a quality test called SMART test first, which is...*

_____

_____

_____

_____

_____

_____

* *In addition, I make sure each of my goals is challenging enough, significant, above my comfort zone, and I track progress toward reaching the finish line by...*

_____

_____

_____

_____

_____

_____

* *I need nontoxic company along the way, and this will consist primarily of the following people...*

_____

_____

_____

_____

_____

_____

*   *I deal with critics along the way in the following way...*

_____

_____

_____

_____

_____

*   *My goals in the area of family are...business/professional life are...hobbies are...family are...*

_____

_____

_____

_____

_____

_____

Twelve

NOWING®
in a Nutshell

To consider NOWING® a quick-fix approach that can change your life 180 degrees within a day is absolutely unrealistic. But what if you would like to experience the first set of positive improvements? What if there were only twenty-four hours that you allow for NOWING® to show you it works and brings ideas and real benefits? Where should you start, then? What would be the most important thing you should work on? How could you fit everything into your current busy life?

Many of my clients come up with these questions once they understand the principles of NOWING® and the details behind the six elements: NEST, ORGANIZE, WORK, INTERACT, NURTURE, GOAL.

There is a way of dealing with all six NOWING® elements that has proven to work well in the past. This requires frequent personal interaction and time to reflect with a professionally trained NOWING® specialist. Therefore, I am happy to spend time each year with a select group of individuals who are ready to embark on this journey toward their dream of a high-performing and healthy life with my personal help. Over the course of this program, I work with each and every individual personally and provide a load of checklists, activities, and exercises to help work through the NOWING® Formula in the best and most efficient way possible. If you are interested in joining this high performers' program, let me know at braininspa.com.

Unfortunately, not all of us will get to meet, and I might not have the pleasure of working with everybody who finds the NOWING® Formula useful. Nevertheless, it is my intention to help you as much as I can even if we have no personal interaction. Therefore, many of the previous chapters have practical activities ready to be incorporated into your life and a set of core questions at the end of each chapter in the "Checkpoint" sections. Make sure you go back to each chapter and answer the questions or complete the exercises, so you get the most out of this book. Also make sure you download your free workbook, including exercise sheets for each NOWING® chapter at braininspa.com. This practical booklet will support you over the course of reading this book and help to bring structure to the exercises.

Still, there are people who just need a jump-start, a "best of" summary for the most essential lessons of the NOWING® Formula. For you I have created this twenty-four-hour-of-NOWING® summary. It is supposed to be a convenient exercise to improve your daily personal performance and productivity and still remain in—or start with—a healthier lifestyle in the digital economy.

This chapter is not about going on a full-scale transformational journey with the help of NOWING® but rather about going for a one-day hike on this journey, in which we pack as many useful things into our backpack as possible.

So let's get started on our one-day trip:

6:30 a.m.	Get up and do your morning ritual to remind you of your purpose, your goal, and your plan for today; drink some water, and do not touch your e-mail. Do a small workout.
7:30 a.m.	Enjoy a healthy breakfast with organic fruits and whole grains, ideally with the company of loved ones; go to your workplace, which reflects a high "you-ish" factor (see the chapter on NEST).
8:30 a.m.	Plan your day with the help of the daily focus sheet; focus on your "tennis balls" and not the "marbles"; arrange your day according to your chronobiological order; plan for breaks.

9:00 a.m.	Productive time working on your "tennis balls" (see the chapter on ORGANIZE).
10:00 a.m.	First e-mail check.
10:30 a.m.	Productive time working on your "tennis balls" (see the chapter on ORGANIZE).
12:00 p.m.	Lunchtime away from your place of work, with good company and some fresh air.
1:00 p.m.	Enjoy some you time, which you use for doing something you like (sports, talk to positive people, and practice some mindfulness).
1:30 p.m.	Continue with your work; plan for breaks for every twenty-five to thirty minutes.
3:00 p.m.	Second e-mail check.
3:30 p.m.	Go for a bigger break, and have a cup of green tea with a friend or coworker; make sure you have something to smile about; do or watch something funny.

3:50 p.m.	Continue your planned work-related activities for today according to your daily focus sheet; remind yourself of being present, being in the moment, and interacting with others by honoring and appreciating them.
5:30 p.m.	Finish your workday and go home.
6:00 p.m.	Enjoy social time with friends—for example, an after-work event, going to the gym, or doing some volunteer work.
7:00 p.m.	Plan for a light organic dinner, which you cook yourself and eat at least three hours before you go to sleep.
8:00 p.m.	Spend time on nonwork-related goals, such as studying, reading, or simply relaxing your way; reserve time for your brain-muscle workout by nurturing your mind.
9:30 p.m.	Reflect on the day and write down your accomplishments or say them out loud; list the things you have completed and not the ones that didn't get done.

10:00 p.m.   Start your bedtime routine.

11:00 p.m.   Go to sleep and enjoy seven or eight
                    hours of true rest.

Thirteen

Ready for takeoff...

If you have made it to this page, there is only one thing I want to say: congratulations. You are hopefully inspired by the NOWING® Formula to start your personal transformation journey to more clarity, productivity, motivation, success, and energy in the digital era. To make progress toward living a joyful life, coming closer to your dream life, is not a bumpy road anymore with lots of question marks along the way.

Now is your time. You have all it takes to get your fundamentals right and optimize your social backbone and your physical environment. You know about the importance of your rituals and habits and how to live true to your creative ambitions. You enjoy more clarity in your life with a focus on the really important things, going from confusion to straight priorities, solving distraction, and mastering organization. You are aware of the optimal challenge-skill balance leading to a flow state, with pro-activity and bold decisions, taking on a true leadership role in the digital industry. You understand the secrets for being more influential, persuasive, and inspiring for others in order to achieve your dreams and allow innovative ideas to emerge. You have the concepts in place to feed your body and your brain along the four dimensions of motion, food, presence, and cognition. Last but not least, you gained clarity for your life's purpose and your true passion, and you are clear about your goals as well as how you can reach them.

But you wouldn't read all these pages if you weren't committed to real success, to making a real difference, and to enjoying every day of your precious life. It's this drive to improve and to make progress that some of us have and some still need to develop. If we don't move on, we don't make progress, and we risk falling behind—and nobody wants that.

Applying the NOWING® Formula with all its ideas, concepts, exercises, and activities hopefully helped you avoid falling behind and allowed you to catch up, to make a first step, maybe a first giant leap in the direction you want. The journey you just started is a challenge, regardless of where you take off from. If you come across a difficult section on this hiking trail, here are my favorite seven directives that keep me going when the going gets tough—and they are easy to remember:

I believe I can do it. Although the average person goes by the saying "seeing is believing," the successful person understands the power of imagination: you can see with your "inner eyes" how it will be once you succeed. So I believe in myself first, which fuels my motivation to get active.

Be precise and focused. Based on your mission, your passion, and your goals, be clear and very precise about what you want. Stick with one theme/place/industry/target group first; dig deeper and not broader. Too many people with a lot of drive would not consider themselves very patient. So instead of hanging in there, digging deeper, and showing some persistence, they move on too quickly. It is always better to finish what you have started first and stay on the initially planned course, even when the going gets a bit tougher; don't give distraction and procrastination a chance.

Go public with your vision. When we have our goals, our ambitions, and our journey developed, many of us tend to make it a private, almost secret endeavor. But vocalizing your goals makes a difference. It will help you attract resources you might need along the way; any publicly announced commitment is so much more powerful, and you will be held accountable for achieving it not only by yourself but by the informed public as well—it's absolutely powerful; believe me.

Stay away from toxic people. If you are surrounded by colleagues, business partners, friends, or even family members who don't support you, who don't believe in you and your objectives, and who project negative energy onto you, make sure the amount of time you spend with them is reduced to the bare minimum, which is not to say canceled completely. When I did a thorough scan through my social backbone some years ago, I had a few wow moments and since then have reduced the contact with some of those negativity projectors to the absolute minimum, including people from my own family. Why? Was it too harsh and rude to do this? No, not at all, because I am responsible for my life and my health, and there is absolutely nobody else who should be given power and control over me, my life, my objectives, and my progress. Also, be careful about how your own language affects your behavior—negativity can also come from the words you frequently choose; the thoughts you allow into your mind; all the criticizing, complaining, and whining that you might be doing all day long about anything that annoys you. Stop it; it won't lead you anywhere and only takes useful energy from you and your goals.

Takeoff can be tough. You have probably been on a plane at least once in your life. Remember all the shaking and rocking during takeoff, the bumpy road into the sky till the plane has reached cruising altitude and then—bad weather aside—everything is smooth and silent? Yes. Apply this experience to any new endeavor you start: the first steps toward your dream might be the toughest ones ever, the most uncomfortable ones, the ones that make you really sweat and hit your limits. But once mastered, this experience is invaluable; it makes you strong and ready for this ride and for any more difficult journey afterward. Frequently leaving your comfort zone is what differentiates highly successful people from the mediocre crowd of the majority.

No plan B. A quote I kept in mind when I started my own company was not to have a plan B because it distracts from plan A. If you internalize the power of this, you will see that failure is not an option. There is no more sneaking out; there is only hanging in there, getting it done, and working really hard without taking the path of least resistance. If you force yourself to succeed with plan A because you wouldn't even know what to do since you have no plan B, it is like having your back against the wall—once that happens, you unleash almost-unknown power within you that allows you to do truly incredible things.

One step a day. Rome wasn't built in day, and the same is true for your next goal or your overall vision: it takes time, but you should make each and every day a step in the right direction; improve just a little bit every twenty-four hours. Tomorrow should be a bit better than yesterday, and if you apply this simple goal in all areas of your life, you will have a lot of achievements that you can look back on after just one year—not to mention if you continue for years two, three, four, or beyond.

I feel truly honored that our paths have crossed and that I had the privilege to share my passion and some of my personal insights with you. I will continue to learn, as we are all supposed to be students first, so never stop exploring something new each day. I am looking forward to seeing you again along this journey. Reach out to me; let's connect and let me know how you are doing. I truly hope that the NOWING® Formula has helped you take a big step toward your dream of maximizing your professional performance and staying healthy in today's digital era.

Let us realize that it is the moment that counts. Not the
YESTERDAY.
Not the TOMORROW.
But the NOW.

About the author

M ichaela Lindinger is the creator of the NOWING® Formula, a strategy used internationally by young professionals looking to maximize their performance and improve their health in the digital industry. She is the founder and CEO of brain in spa, the first platform for performance and health in the digital industry, helping millennial talents, start-ups, and innovative organizations gain more clarity, influence, productivity, resilience, and success.

Michaela is also a board member at an interdisciplinary, innovative health-services organization for professionals, executives, and entire organizations. As an inspiring young woman with ten-plus years of experience in international management positions responsible for strategy, digital value creation, and innovation, she received a leadership award for visionary leadership at the age of twenty-eight. Her proven NOWING® Formula for achieving healthy performance in the midst of the digital industrial revolution is reinventing how young professionals around the world can enjoy a charged life more effectively and efficiently and with more engagement, with formats that fit a digital lifestyle.

Michaela is an experienced management consultant and intrapreneur; a member of the international Forbes® Coaches Council; an in-demand keynote speaker and productivity trainer; and an executive performance coach, blogger, and author. She serves her clients as a neutral yet professional and experienced companion with guidance, proven tools, and hands-on approaches.

Additionally, she has worked as a lecturing professor for undergraduate and graduate courses at an Austrian University since the age of twenty-nine and is a member of the International Society for Coaching Psychology. Michaela is one of those authentic, millennial women who enjoy the golden path between high professional performance, a personal focus on her health, and the beauty of a private life being married and a mom to a wonderful daughter.

Michaela holds an international business master's degree from the University of Applied Sciences of Upper Austria and a master's degree in coaching psychology from the University of East London.

Meet Michaela at braininspa.com and get free additional resources and training material.

CONNECT WITH MICHAELA LINDINGER
Twitter: @braininspa
Facebook: facebook.com/braininspa
LinkedIn: https://at.linkedin.com/in/michaelalindinger
Blog: braininspa.com/blog

Note to the reader

The material and content provided by Michaela Lindinger and braininspa.com contain the opinions and ideas of the founder and author. It is intended to provide helpful and informative material on the subjects addressed. Any strategies, activities, or tools outlined may not be suitable for every individual and are not guaranteed or warranted to produce particular results. The reader understands and agrees that neither the author nor her representatives are engaged in rendering legal, financial, accounting, psychotherapeutic, medical, or other professional advice or service. It is highly encouraged that the reader consult a professional before adopting any of the suggestions if unsure. There is no warranty made with respect to the accuracy or completeness of the information or references contained herein, and brain in spa as well as any representatives specifically disclaim any responsibility for any liability, loss, or risk, personal or otherwise, which is incurred as a consequence, directly or indirectly, of the use and application of any of the contents provided by brain in spa and Michaela Lindinger.

The views expressed in this book and its foreword are those of the authors and not those of the Universities of Cambridge and East London, or Empsy, Cambridge Coaching Psychology Group.